MANAGE YOUR FEAR. BEFORE IT MANAGES YOU.

THE ANXIOUS CONGREGATION

KEN THIESSEN

Published by Power of One Publishing

Power of One Publishing
979 Gull Road
Regina, SK. S4N 7S1
CANADA

ISBN 978-0-9880396-0-5
Copyright © 2012 Ken Thiessen

Cover design by Go Giraffe Go Writing & Design Inc, Regina, SK. CANADA

Cover artwork by Jeremiah Morelli, www.morjers-art.de

All rights reserved. No part of this book may be reproduced, stored in a retrieval system or transmitted in any form or by any means without the prior written permission of Ken Thiessen.

For information on Power of One Consulting, visit the website, www.powerofoneconsulting.ca

Unless otherwise indicated, all Scripture quotations are taken from the Holy Bible, New Living Translation, copyright © 1996, 2004, 2007 by Tyndale House Foundation. Used by permission of Tyndale House Publishers, Inc., Carol Stream, Illinois 60188. All rights reserved.

DEDICATION

To Eric, Larry, and Paul - fellow hobbits in the shire of life. Your friendship means more to me than you will ever know. I am the beneficiary of your passionate desire to love God and love others. By word and deed you encourage and prod me to keep responding to Jesus' "follow me" call to passionately love God and other people.

CONTENTS

	Acknowledgments	i
1	Introduction	1
2	Grenwich - A "Normal" Congregation	8
3	"Follow Me and Change Your World" - Jesus	16
4	Grenwich - "Following Who?"	31
5	Measuring What Matters - To Jesus	40
6	Grenwich - What We Measure "Matters"!	56
7	The Main Thing - Loving God and Loving People	69
8	Grenwich - What's Love Got To Do With It?	82
9	The Language of Love Includes "Yes" AND "No"	94
10	Grenwich - Framing a New Paradigm	110
11	"Would You Like to Get Well?"	120
12	Grenwich - Living Into the New Paradigm	136
13	The Change Process - Risk and Learning; Faith and Courage!	148
14	The Anxious Congregation Rehab Regimen	159
15	Grenwich - Congregational Redesign	172
16	Every Part Doing Its Part	181
17	Grenwich - Still Anxious But Self-Aware	197
18	Your Congregation - On Mission With God	207
19	Grenwich - An Update	212
	About the Author	215

ACKNOWLEDGMENTS

How does one adequately begin to recognize the people who have been instrumental in shaping the thoughts which comprise the book you are about to read? It's a perilous and risky journey for sure. The danger is that you will overlook someone who deserves both recognition and gratitude. What follows is my humble and best attempt. My apologies up front to those who rightly should be included. Any oversight is completely unintentional.

When what you do vocationally brings a profound sense of enjoyment, fulfillment, and satisfaction, you're a pretty lucky person. I'm grateful to God for the gifts he's given me, the people he has sent my way to help shape and mold me into the image of his son Jesus Christ, and the privilege of trying to make a small difference through the ministry opportunities that come my way.

To all who have read through the manuscript and offered your input and perspective, thank you so much for your willingness to make the investment of time and energy in this project. A special thanks to Mark Buchanan for your encouragement to develop the initial book proposal into a fuller manuscript. Your help in the early stages served as a catalyst propelling me on this literary journey. Lisa, your investment of time, talent and resource in editing the manuscript has been significant! You are gifted and skilled, and this project is the beneficiary of your work.

Mom and Dad, thanks for the gift of life, for grounding me in a family where love for others and love for God was modelled and encouraged. You have always accepted me as I am, you have given me wings to fly, and encouraged me to follow God's call in my life, even when it meant moving away from family. Bev, Joel and Carissa are also the beneficiaries of your unconditional love and acceptance!

I would have never embarked on the vocational journey of pastoral ministry were it not for two pastors who saw something in me and called it out of me. Henry Willms and Abe Block saw ministry gifting and potential and urged me to pursue formal training and engage ministry. Without their encouragement, mentorship, and support, I doubt I would have chosen the course I did.

Ken Thiessen

I was fortunate to have college and seminary professors who embraced me as a peer, not just a student. Martin Lewadny, Ed Neufeld, Steve Masterson, and Don Sawatzky modelled what they taught, helped me reflect on theology and life, and taught me how to integrate the two! I am indebted to each of them for their part in my spiritual formation.

Who would have thought that a Pentecostal Edmonton Oilers fan and a Baptist Calgary Flames fan could look beyond theological differences and intense sports rivalries to become good friends and maintain that friendship over the span of many years and thousands of miles! Marty Mittelstadt has been an ongoing source of theological stimulation and inspiration and to think it all started because we skipped out on seminary chapels to build a friendship that has served to spur us on to love and good deeds!

Larry Robideau, Paul Spate and Eric Thielmann have been accountability partners and friends in ways that truly go beyond words. In their own way each has supported, encouraged, and motivated me to keep going in the journey of faith and life!

Dr. Craig Van Gelder has been a special mentor and become a good friend. He helped me develop and hone my consulting skills and has been an encouraging, supportive cheerleader in the process! His skill at inviting theological reflection has been instrumental in my ongoing spiritual formation and practise of ministry.

Lloyd Alstad, a ministry colleague, deserves special mention. In many ways I cut my ministry teeth as associate pastor under Lloyd's watch. We are as different as night is from day, but we knew that we were stronger together than we were alone. We found a way (most days) to recognize and affirm what the other brought to the mix in terms of ministry gifting and perspective. Countless staff meetings and innumerable cups of coffee at Salsbury House in Winnipeg have borne fruit all these many years later!

I would be remiss if I failed to recognize my deep debt of gratitude to Dr. Mark Davies. He did his best to discourage me from taking his course "Understanding Congregations as Systems", and for good reason. However, he yielded to my stubborn persistence and one course turned into a doctoral project and a good friendship. Mark, your encouragement, support, affirmation, patience, and cheerleading through the process of supervising my doctoral project are so appreciated! You told me what I needed to hear, not always what I wanted to hear. You pushed me to be better, to continue to think and reflect on organizational life from a systems perspective. Your fingerprints are woven into every page that follows.

Last and most importantly, a project such as this never comes together without the support and encouragement of family. Joel and Carissa, you have done your dad proud as you have faced the challenges of growing up in a pastor's home. Your love and support along the way have been so appreciated. You have married well and I have inherited a great son-in-law and a great daughter-in-law. Scott and Helen, you are truly a part of the family and your love and support are deeply appreciated.

Bev, what can I say? Through 31+ years of marriage you have supported me along the journey of our life together. Even though you vowed you would never marry a pastor, (and I wasn't one when we got married) you have paid the price of being a pastor's wife. Through our time in college and seminary you were a support to me and the kids! You were there to encourage and support me when I embarked on my Doctor of Ministry studies. You have never wavered in your support for me, my calling, and my gifting. When I made the choice to step out on my own and start my consulting practice you were there to support and encourage me. Your affirmation years ago that I would one day write a book has now finally come true. The fact that you still love to hear me preach continues to amaze me. You are my friend, my lover, my soulmate!

Ken Thiessen

Ken Thiessen

Chapter 1
Introduction

Is your congregation an anxious congregation? If it was, how would you know? What if it was and you didn't realize it? What criteria would you use to frame your response?

My experience as a pastor, denominational leader, and organizational consultant has shown me that all congregations are in fact "anxious." They're driven more by fear than faith, driven more by fear than love. Fear of how others will respond. Fear of how they will be perceived and received by others. Fear of the price they will have to pay to question or stand up to the status quo. Fear that they might lose face, or be rejected in the context of church life. Fear that others might be upset and get angry. Fear of being wrong. Fear of being right. For church staff, the fear of losing a source of livelihood, and with it the ability to provide for them and their family, influences many of their decisions, and in some cases, most of their decisions. Anxious congregations are fearful congregations. Fear shapes most relationships and influences most decisions, oftentimes subconsciously or unconsciously.

As a result most congregations are completely unaware of how that lurking anxiety and fear impacts and significantly hampers their ability to live out God's call to join him in mission! To suggest that anxiety is "alive and well" in their respective congregation would be met with a confused, blank stare from many pastors and church leaders. They have become so used to the latent systemic anxiety that it feels "normal." Many would in fact define their experience as "normal" and assume they're doing reasonably well. "Oh we have a few challenges but we're managing them reasonably well! We're no worse off than any other church!" Some would even say, "Our church is growing, our attendance is up, our giving is strong! How can you say we're an 'anxious' congregation?"

What fears plague and haunt you? What fears keep you from fully engaging in the life of your congregation as you live out God's call to love him and love other people? What are the fears that drive the congregation you're a part of, influencing important decisions and diminishing the quality of community life? Do you ever secretly worry that all of the activities and programs might "go off the rails"? Do you feel the pressure to keep it going and secretly fear that maybe you don't have what it takes? Do you ever find yourself wondering whether people would still like you (and follow you if you're a pastor or church leader) if they REALLY knew who you were? If you do, how does that impact the way in which you engage relationships? Do you worry about people leaving your church? Or about the conflict that's simmering just under the surface of congregational life? That's anxiety! Underlying the anxiety is a fear that acts as a fuel source for an already burning fire!

No matter how much you have an intellectual understanding of Scripture's exhortation to "be anxious for nothing" and "fear not", latent (and sometimes not so latent) anxiety and fear exerts a powerful influence on the dynamics of life in most local congregations. Okay, it exerts its influence on every local congregation, your congregation. Some are just more attuned to its presence and its impact. To the degree that a local congregation is unaware of the anxiety present or is unable to effectively manage the fear that fuels it, to that degree it is hampered from being all it could be in living out the call to love God and love each other.

In his compelling book, **The Anxious Organization. Why Smart Companies Do Dumb Things,** Jeffrey Miller suggests that, "Any living organism that is not anxious is on its way to being extinct. In everything that lives, anxiety is a fundamental expression of the survival instinct."[1] As I read that statement for the first time, Miller had my attention and I was propelled on a reflective journey contemplating systemic organizational anxiety, specifically in the context of the local church.

While Miller directs his focus to business organizations, what struck me were the direct parallels between the realities in a business context and those of local churches. For some of you, the fact I have drawn a straight line connection between organizational experiences of business and the church has already begun to increase the level of your anxiety. Some of you may be headed down the road of writing me off because of it. "The church is not a business and should not be run like a business" is a refrain I have often heard. But bear with me, hear me out. What if you are in fact a part of an "anxious" congregation? More importantly, and probably more difficult to consider, what if you are an anxious person whose fears shape more of your actions and reactions than what you're currently aware of? What then?

Let me be really clear about one more thing. "Anxious" is a descriptive term not a prescriptive term. I'm not saying your particular congregation is "bad" because you are "anxious". I'm not saying you are a bad person, leader, or pastor because

---

[1] Jeffrey A Miller, The Anxious Organization. Why Smart Companies Do Dumb Things. (Tempe, AZ: Facts on Demand Press, 2002), 2

you're "anxious". I'm simply describing a reality without making any evaluative judgment at all. So I think no less of you or your congregation because of the descriptor. However, the less that anxiety and fear is understood and clearly articulated, the more it holds you and your congregation captive, limiting your ability to fully join God in mission. It's operating like a virus that threatens to overtake you and wreak havoc unless you begin to develop better ways to manage the anxiety and fear. But learning to better manage the fear and anxiety is only the beginning of the cure. To be honest, there is no cure. It's not like one day you'll wake up and realize you're no longer anxious and you'll never be fearful again! It's not going to happen! But you can live life managing your anxiety in much better ways and that is significant progress.

Now lest you think I just want to stir the pot, I know the pain of the journey, because that's my story. As I embarked on my own reflective process, I began to realize that I was in fact the pastor of an anxious congregation. They would never have used the word "anxious" to self-describe but it was in fact their reality. I would never have used the word "anxious" to describe them either. It's been the reality of every church I've had the privilege to serve as pastor.

But here's the shocking piece. I came to realize that I was an anxious pastor leading an anxious congregation! If you were to observe me in my leadership role in that congregation, most of you would never use the word "anxious" to describe me. I project a sense of calm control and composure when leading an organization. I know that to be true about myself. But what I also came to realize was that my calm projected persona masked an anxiety and fear that was stirring under the surface exercising more influence and control on my leadership style than I had ever realized or imagined possible! That was a shocking and humbling wake-up call for me!

So I understand the journey I'm inviting you to embark on. I know the fears, apprehensions, uncertainty, and the intimidating territory you're moving into on the journey. I know that some of what you discover will be unsettling, troubling, and frustrating. But I also know the freedom that comes when you can begin to name your own anxiety, own it for what it is, and begin to manage the fear that fuels it in a way that is more God-honouring and authentic. It has the potential to more powerfully and positively impact the lives of others as you seek to live out God's call in your life. It has the potential to transform the way you lead and the way you interact with other anxious, fearful people.

I encourage you to engage this journey as an individual, but more importantly as leadership teams, small groups, or pastoral staff teams. Anxiety may be an individual issue but it never remains an individual issue for long. Anxious, fearful individuals ALWAYS work hard to disperse their anxiety to the rest of the clan! Anxiety is the gift that keeps on giving and giving and giving, and not in a healthy way!

The fact that you've picked up this book and begun reading indicates you have at least some interest in the subject matter. As you embark on this journey, you're going to become a part of Grenwich Community Church. If there is an actual Grenwich Community Church, I apologize up front. I'm not writing about your church! It's a creative fabrication of mine.

In one way or another every individual and every situation you're going to encounter at Grenwich is a real, live person, in a real, live local church context that I've encountered as a pastor, denominational leader, and consultant. Just to be really clear, all of the names have been changed to protect the guilty, and ALL are guilty! That's right, all are guilty! So are you! While you may be shocked or offended that I would make that assessment of you without having met you, that's the good news! Really, it is. Trust me! (My wife is tired of hearing me say that because I say it often!)

Not only are you going to become a part of Grenwich as a congregational system, you're going to be challenged to reflect on the experience of Grenwich as it relates to some of the great themes of Scripture. Themes like loving God and loving other people in the context of local parish life! You'll be invited to wrestle with some of the great questions posed by Jesus. Questions like, "Would you like to get well?" "What do you want me to do for you?" You'll have an opportunity to reflect on Jesus' call, "Follow me!" What does that look like for you as an individual? What does that look like for groups of people like your congregation who come together around a shared belief desiring to make a significant difference in your community, in the world?

So I invite you to embark on a journey. If you find your heart beating a little faster, a sweat starting to break out, just be honest and name it for what it is. That's fear! That's anxiety! Now that you know what it is, you have a choice as to what you are going to do in response. Is your fear and anxiety going to control and immobilize you or are you going to set out on this journey, face your fears and take your anxiety along with you? The only thing you have to worry about is taking the first step. Once you've successfully done that then focus on the next step, and then the next, and the next, and the next! Before you know it you will have begun the process of managing your fear before it manages you and defines you as an anxious person or an anxious congregation!

Come along on the journey knowing that you're not alone; others have gone before you. But even more importantly, the God whom you love and serve is with you! What's uncertain and fearful to you, is known and adventurous to him! He really does have your best interests at heart! Let's talk more on the other side! I'm looking forward to hearing your story!

For Reflection and Discussion

1. In your own words, how would you define an "anxious" congregation?

2. What would you say are some of the marks of an "anxious" congregation?

3. What indicators do you see that might suggest your congregation is "anxious"?

4. In what ways do you think you enable anxiety and fear to function in unhealthy ways in your congregation?

5. Describe a situation where you felt anxious and afraid. How did you respond in that situation? What did you learn about managing anxiety and fear based on that situation?

6. As you embark on this journey, how would you describe your mood? Afraid? Apprehensive? Hopeful? Excited? Why do you think that is?

Chapter 2
Grenwich - A "Normal" Congregation

Grenwich Community Church was a relatively typical congregation engaged in ministry in a small, vibrant, and growing community. Situated just twenty minutes from a city of 60,000 and halfway between two metropolitan regions each with a population in excess of one million, a ninety minute drive east or west gave access to big box stores, fine dining, cultural events, major airports, and world class professional sporting events. So as much as Grenwich was situated in a picturesque and somewhat quaint community, the urban influence was pronounced and real.

Grenwich's beginnings were humble, the fruit of a passionate sense of God's call to a handful of people; a call to plant a congregation eighty years earlier. Over the first seventy-five years of its history, they had enjoyed a relatively stable experience as a congregation of God's people, growing to seventy-five worshipers on an average Sunday morning. For almost thirty years, the founding lay person, a local business professional, had provided pastoral leadership before the congregation called its first full time pastor. His six year tenure was the shortest of any pastor in the church's history, but still quite respectable by most standards. Seven, fourteen, and nine year tenures characterized the pastors who followed. Then, in the seventy-fifth year of its history, the congregation made a decision, the impact of which would dramatically change the course of its life and ministry in this community of 8,000.

Eight hundred miles to the east, Barry Moffat was ministering in a larger urban setting. Having served eight years as associate pastor in a multi-staff context he was restless, sensing God calling him to a ministry situation where his gifts could be more fully utilized in new and growing ways. Barry's restlessness wasn't an angry fight with God or the church. It was the result of a prolonged dialogue with key leaders in his church, his senior pastor, and other trusted confidants. Each had affirmed Barry's giftedness and readiness to move into a Lead Pastor role. Barry's leadership involvements beyond his local church context had also served to give him additional ministry and leadership experience as well as raise his profile beyond his current ministry setting.

Barry never anticipated that his restless search would lead him to a church like Grenwich! Given his visionary leadership style and ministry philosophy, he always anticipated (even planned!) a move to another urban setting. So when David Hill, the chair of Grenwich's Pastoral Search Committee came calling, Barry was somewhat taken aback. He knew relatively little about the church or community apart from who the previous pastor had been. That initial, exploratory conversation with David led to subsequent phone conversations and an exchange of information about the church and the community. Six weeks later Barry was on his way to meet some of the people of Grenwich and the community where it sought to live out God's call to ministry.

Barry arrived with limited expectations. Why should he expect anything? He already had it all figured out. God was going to call him to lead a congregation in a large urban setting and this certainly didn't fit the profile! But he would "check it out".

He had never met David Hill in spite of David's prominent leadership role in the denomination. David had indicated that he would meet Barry at the airport wearing a John Deere jacket. That would be the "sign". Coming down the escalator to the luggage carousel, Barry laid eyes on a 60ish grey haired man wearing the infamous John Deere jacket.

David fit Barry's stereotype of a small town church leader. A seasoned looking farmer, David's personality in some ways matched his appearance. He wasn't the most socially adept person Barry had met. He was pleasant enough, but somewhat rough and gruff around the edges with some strong opinions!

The ninety minute drive from the airport was filled with small talk which served to help Barry and David get to know a little bit more about each other and the community which David had called home for his entire life! As Barry engaged David in conversation, he wasn't quite sure that what he encountered on the outside was in fact the real thing. David said a lot of the right things but beneath the veneer there seemed to be something that rang hollow. While it was much too early to make those kinds of generalizations, Barry made a mental note of it, committed to fully engage the process with as open a mind as possible.

As Barry was given the tour of the community and surrounding area, he was surprised at how quickly he was taken in by his experience. Surrounded by rolling hills and farms, the community had a warm and inviting feel to it. In some ways, it reminded Barry of the town he'd grown up in, without the mountains.

It had a strong mixture of industry and agriculture which provided a diverse economic base. What surprised Barry was the number of recreational vehicle and automobile dealerships. This was obviously not an economically deprived or depressed community. People could afford some of the luxuries of life! The community was comprised of some well-kept older areas and a growing number of new housing developments, giving an indication of its economic prosperity. Only later would Barry discover that this community was situated in one of the most prosperous corridors on the continent.

As Barry was brought to the church property, he was again impressed. Located on a major traffic route, the church was set on a generous sized piece of property. The building, while modest, reflected thoughtful planning with opportunity for facility expansion incorporated into the design.

What most surprised Barry was the fact that this church had no pews, something which shattered another of his stereotypes. Revealing his bias Barry asked, "So when did you get rid of your pews?" "We've never had pews!" was David's response leaving Barry somewhat taken aback.

Before Barry had time to process his internal reaction twenty-two four year-old children exploded in a somewhat orderly fashion into the "sanctuary". Barry was informed that this was the local community pre-school who had been using the church facility for the past twenty years. Operated by an independent board not associated with the church, every child who attended play-school in the community entered the doors of Grenwich Community Church! The more he engaged the process, the more his eyes were being opened to ministry potential and possibilities. As a visionary he was shocked to find what he deemed to be a deep desire to join God in mission demonstrated by this small town congregation.

As he met the Search Committee for the first time he was impressed with the demographic diversity on the Committee.

There were long time church members and relative newcomers, professional and blue collar people, men and women, single and married, younger and older people. Barry would continue to have his preconceived notions exposed and shattered!

As he had reviewed the documentation sent to him in preparation for his visit, Barry had been pleasantly surprised to discover that Grenwich had done some significant work in articulating and crafting their sense of vision and mission! They had a vision to reach out to their community in new and fresh ways, seemingly unhindered by the traditions of their seventy-five year history. The church had worked through issues like vision and mission and even had much of it written down and approved by the congregation. They had identified ministry goals in some areas that were important to Barry. To be honest, Barry was shocked! His assumption was that it was unusual for a larger urban church to have done this kind of work, and non-existent in small town congregations like Grenwich. Yet another step in the process of dismantling his bias!

Members of the Search Committee were keen to know how Barry would specifically engage with and involve himself in the community, something which was germane to his philosophy of ministry. As he shared his vision for community involvement and outreach, their excitement seemed to grow. Sharing his desire to be relevant and contemporary in his preaching, they seemed undaunted by his innovative creativity. At least that's what he sensed, and they gave him no reason to question that. He left that first meeting feeling something stirring deep within him, a dream of what could be, both for him and for this community of faith.

Back home, Barry's wife Diane and their two children were anxiously waiting to hear news as to how his visit was going.

Diane did not expect anything to materialize from this visit, sharing many of Barry's preconceived notions. In some ways it felt like God was teasing them with something that really had little chance of materializing.

So when Barry arrived back home with the news that the Pastoral Search Committee wanted him to return for a second visit WITH Diane, she was shocked. She was even more stunned to discover that Barry was open to it, and even excited about the ministry possibilities! She had been convinced that Barry would return and confirm her suspicions that this would not be a ministry fit for them. She too was convinced they would be moving to a large urban setting, not a smaller community and not a smaller community church! Barry assured her that this was not your ordinary small town church! At least so he thought.

The return visit a month later went equally well, although Barry was somewhat apprehensive, not quite sure how Diane would respond. The weekend was a low key affair which caught Barry off guard. There was no formal meeting with the congregation, just a series of informal gatherings with individuals and groups from within the congregation – most over a meal, which suited him fine. He thrived in that kind of relational environment.

Before Barry even had a chance to preach in the Sunday morning worship service, Diane confessed that she knew they would be moving to this quaint community, something which also served to shatter Barry's expectations. Diane was a rooted person who wasn't prone to moving, so the strength of her conviction was completely out of character. He filed it away as another important piece of information in the discernment process.

The Sunday morning service went well. Barry preached a strong message and the interactions with people after the service seemed to be another affirmation that this was heading in a positive direction. Before long Barry and Diane were on a plane headed back to suburbia to await the official vote of the congregation which was to take place the following Tuesday.

Anticipating a positive outcome of that vote didn't make the wait any less nerve wracking. It was almost like the juvenile "she loves me, she loves me not" kind of mind game! As they had travelled home and had time to debrief their experience, Barry and Diane had decided that should the church extend a call, they would accept. So when the phone finally rang late Tuesday evening, their emotions were riding the biggest roller coaster imaginable. David Hill informed Barry that the vote to call him as their new Lead Pastor had passed with a ninety percent majority vote of the congregation.

Following some final negotiations surrounding the salary and benefits package, which David assured Barry wouldn't be a problem, Barry accepted the call agreeing to commence ministry later that year. Barry should have noticed that David unilaterally offered up the assurances, but he didn't. He was caught up in the excitement of the ministry potential and opportunity, and the sense of adventure that was about to unfold. Little did Barry and Diane, David, or the members of Grenwich Community Church realize how that decision would impact their lives and their shared ministry.

For Reflection and Discussion

1. What are some of the significant events which have shaped the life of your congregation?

2. Who are some of the key people who have served the congregation? Pastors? Church Leaders?

3. What has been the most painful experience you've gone through as a congregation? What were some of the underlying causes?

4. Has your congregation articulated its sense of vision and mission? How often do you review it? How aware is the overall congregation of your vision and mission?

5. How do your current ministries help you live into your vision and mission? What changes or modifications might better help you realize your vision and mission?

6. If you haven't articulated your sense of vision and mission, why do you think that is?

7. What is God currently doing in your life as a congregation? What does God yet want to do? What stands in the way of that happening?

Ken Thiessen

Chapter 3
"Follow Me and Change Your World" - Jesus

Does the story of Grenwich Community Church in any way sound familiar? Probably. Grenwich's story is not all that unique; it's the story of many churches. There are some variations, but the story line is basically the same. It doesn't matter whether it's a small town or a large urban setting, a long-established church or a church plant, a traditional church or a more contemporary, innovative church. People are people, no matter the context. That's not to say that context is irrelevant or unimportant, but human nature demonstrates some predictable patterns.

When a congregation is in the process of searching for a new pastor to provide leadership, assume that anxiety is present. Assume that anxiety is alive and well even if it isn't overtly evident! Anxiety is couched in the search process, the composition of the committee, and particularly in the questions that are asked (or not asked) of potential candidates. They're clues as to where anxiety and fear are present, exerting an influence on the system! Anxiety is particularly acute if the exit of the previous pastor was painful and conflicted.

Here's another assumption you should make. Throughout much of the process the church and the pastoral candidate are each engaged in deception and dishonesty! I know these are designed to be discernment processes where congregations and pastoral candidates listen for the call of God. I sincerely believe that God speaks through these processes and I affirm that there is genuine discernment that takes place. But let's be honest. Both the church and the pastoral candidate are driven as much by fear as faith! If they really knew this about me would they still call me to be their pastor? If she really knew this about us would she still accept a call to serve among us? So rather than walk with integrity and authenticity in the face of the real fear and anxiety, both parties are guarded, allowing their respective fears to control the relational interactions. Only later do they wake up to "reality".

Clues as to how anxiety is at work are also firmly embedded in the formal and informal leadership structures of the congregation and it raises a very important question. Whose lead most influences the direction of the people who comprise a local congregation? Who are they really following? Are they following the lead of the David Hills, and every church has one, or are they truly following the call of God to join him in mission in the community context where they are situated?

Os Guinness suggests that two words more than any other have changed the course of human history - "Follow me!"[2] Reflect on that for a moment as it relates to your life individually or the life of the congregation you're a part of. What I think you'll discover is that Guinness is on to something significant.

Sometimes the "follow me" call is couched in the slick marketing of that "must have – can't live without it" product! Every day, more times than we can count, we are bombarded with the consumerist mantra of "follow me and I'll give what

---

[2] Os Guinness, The Call: Finding and Fulfilling the Central Purpose of Your Life. (Nashville, TN: Thomas Nelson Publishers, 2003)

you don't have!" More often than we care to admit, we follow the Pied Piper of consumerism only to arrive at the destination of disappointment, hopelessness, and emptiness. The call that sounded so appealing ends up with a hollow ring to it! And a bigger price tag!

Virtually every generation can point to a charismatic leader who generated a committed, loyal, and sometimes fanatical following by issuing the call, "follow me!" Every generation has been impacted for better or for worse by that kind of decisive leadership. Some of those leaders have used their persuasive abilities to inspire and empower others to accomplish feats few dreamed possible. Others have used their charisma and personal power to generate a group of followers who in turn oppressed, suppressed, and repressed human effort, dignity, and accomplishment.

Two thousand years ago, a carpenter from Nazareth said to twelve young men, "follow me" and the world has never been the same since. Neither were they! Their priorities and values were transformed and their life direction forever altered.

Since you're reading this book, I'm going to assume that at one level or another you profess some degree of loyalty to Jesus and you're committed to following him more closely. Why not consider what Jesus' call to "follow me" might have meant to that first group of people who responded, and then allow me to outline what it might look like if we took it more seriously in the context of the local church.

Jesus' call to those twelve young men is recorded in each of the Gospels but Mark's record reads as follows: "One day as Jesus was walking along the shore of the Sea of Galilee, he saw Simon and his brother Andrew throwing a net into the water, for they fished for a living. Jesus called out to them, 'Come, follow me, and I will show you how to fish for people!' And they left their nets at once and followed him. A little farther up the shore Jesus saw Zebedee's sons, James and John, in a boat repairing their nets. He called them at once, and they also followed him, leaving their father, Zebedee, in the boat with the hired men." (Mark 1:16-20)

"Follow Me" Involves Radically Altering Your Priorities

The danger we face is glossing over the significance of what is being communicated in these verses because the words are so familiar to us. Many of us know what they say. We know the story.

But as you reflect on Mark's record of Jesus' call what you notice is the urgency in terms of the response. The call to follow resulted in an immediate response that was radical and decisive – they walked off the job! Think about that for a moment. When was the last time someone said to you, "follow me" and you dropped everything and went with them? Immediately! Left behind everything that you and others would consider to be important, even essential to stable, healthy, "normal" everyday life. Nowadays if you did that, your friends would be admitting you into the psychiatric ward of your local hospital.

In each of the Gospel records we see that Jesus' call was so compelling and irresistible that these fishermen left everything, and did so immediately! They didn't leave some things; they didn't leave most things; they left everything! Whatever prior claims had captured their life focus and attention immediately lost their appeal and validity.

Was it because their lives to that point had been so terrible? If that was the case, then you might be able to explain it away. However you try to explain it, what is unmistakable is that these young men left everything! Their father, the hired servants, the nets, the boat! All were left behind as they committed themselves wholeheartedly to follow Jesus. That begs the question: Who was this man who called them? Who was this man whose call was so compelling they would abandon everything in response?

The call to follow Jesus meant that each of them had to radically alter the priorities and values which had shaped the trajectory of their lives to that point in time. It appears they made that adjustment without hesitation, reservation, or apparent struggle. I suspect that if you're at all like me, you'd make those kinds of core alterations to your life if you knew that the changes would somehow make your life easier, more efficient, more enjoyable. Instead of their lives getting easier, responding to the "follow me" call meant life would get harder for these twelve young men – there would be great personal cost attached to their decision.

It wouldn't surprise me if that makes you a bit uncomfortable. It makes me uncomfortable. I wish it wasn't so. Where we try to sugar-coat the cost of following Jesus, he didn't. He never shied away from letting others know what the cost would be and the twelve would find out soon enough what it would cost them personally. Listen to Jesus' response to an interested observer, "Another of his disciples said, 'Lord, first let me return home and bury my father.' But Jesus told him, 'Follow me now. Let the spiritually dead bury their own dead.'" (Matthew 18:20-22) There's no sugar coating there, no political correctness. Just the straight goods!

Every one of us has responded to the "follow me" call. Individually we have responded and collectively as we come together in local congregations we've responded. The question is, "Whose call have we responded to?" Whose invitation has been so compelling that we have abandoned all other claims on our life to embrace that call?

If someone were able to objectively evaluate you on the basis of the priorities that consume your energy and life focus, whose call would they say has been so compelling and irresistible to you? Is it the call of materialism which promises happiness and contentment with the accumulation of material resources and possessions? Is it the call of escapism which promises relief from the pressures of life by numbing the emptiness you feel with excessive reliance on drugs, alcohol, work, sex, X-Box, Wii, social networking, watching television? Is it the call of self-centredness which assures you that there's nothing wrong with focusing on your own needs because "you deserve it"? Is it the call of autonomy which says that you don't need to be accountable to anyone because "you are our own boss!" Is it the call of a pain-free and safe life which would have you believe that it is possible to have that experience if you just control your world enough, if you take no risks, if you adopt a "better safe than sorry" attitude towards life?

Or is it the call of Jesus who said that ultimately you find your life by losing it, you find your life not in living a risk free life but in risking it all, who said that true fulfilment in life is found not in self-centredness but in self-sacrifice and service of others!

To embrace the "follow me" call of Jesus is to radically alter your personal priorities and that will always manifest itself in the way in which you live your life. Any examination and study of the Bible that doesn't lead to concrete behavioural change aborts what God designs the Bible to give birth to. If you are to be true to Jesus' "follow me" call then the goal of that study is not the accumulation of spiritual information. The goal is spiritual formation and transformation!

Whose call have you responded to in your local church community? If someone were able to objectively assess and evaluate the priorities that consume your energy and focus as a church, whose call would they say has been so compelling that you couldn't resist it? Is it the call that suggests you can focus all your energies only on those who are a part of the church, particularly those who have built the church and are the long-term "members" as if the church were an exclusive country club? Is it the call that invites you to insulate yourself from the realities of that world "out there"; that world that's got so many social problems, and that doesn't share or embrace your values?

Or is it the call of Jesus? By his own lifestyle and example he illustrated that living out God's call is about neither insulating nor sheltering yourself from the world; it's not about focusing only on yourself. It's about engaging your world in such a way so as to be salt and light. It's about focusing not only on the blessing that is yours as fellow heirs of God's covenant with Abraham. It's also about the second half of the covenant with Abraham, that of being a blessing to the communities in which God has placed your congregation.

Describing the church that has understood the "follow me" call of Jesus, Scott McKnight says this: "It does not invite people to church but instead wanders into the world as the church. It asks its community 'How can we help you?' instead of knocking on doors to increase membership. In other words, it becomes a community with open windows and open doors and sees Sunday morning as the opportunity to prepare for a week of service to the community, asking not how many are attending the services but what redemptive traits are we seeing in our community. It wants to embody a life that is other-oriented rather than self-oriented, that is community-directed rather than church-oriented."[3] Whose call have you responded to individually and as a church?

---

[3] http://www.vanguardchurch.com/mck_ec.pdf

"Follow Me" is a Call to Follow In Community

But there's a second aspect to Jesus' "follow me" call. If you were going to start a new movement that was going to take the world by storm and you had the opportunity to pick your own team to make that happen, what kind of people would you choose? What names and faces come to mind? What character qualities would you look for?

Notice the characters Jesus chose. They were a motley crew. You've got Peter who never had a thought he didn't verbalize. Peter's brother Andrew could never extricate himself from living in Peter's shadow. James and John were at times more focused on their own egos and status than they were on following Jesus. Simon the Zealot would rather shoot the local politician than submit to the laws of the land. Matthew, the tax collector, worked for the government and had a reputation similar to your local loan shark. He had a license to steal! For a Jewish person to be employed by the Roman government was one of the worst things you could do! Put him next to Simon the Zealot and watch the fireworks!

You've got guys like Nathaniel, Bartholomew, the other James, Thaddeus, and Philip who just seem to go along with the flow and don't seem to rock the boat. Then there's Thomas who would probably drive most of us to the brink of insanity because he wouldn't believe a thing you said unless you had hard evidence upon hard evidence to answer all of his questions. What about Judas who would turn on you in a heartbeat if there was a dollar in it for him? Can't you just see these guys on a reality TV series? Okay, maybe I'm being a bit hard on them, but not much!

If we're honest with each other, we have to admit they're probably not the people we would choose to turn the world upside down. They wouldn't have chosen each other! But Jesus chose them and said to them, "follow me". Jesus' call to "follow me" brought them together in this unlikely group and it was in the context of their life together that they learned more fully what it really meant to "follow me" the way Jesus envisioned it.

Isn't that the way it is in the church? Your church? You find yourself connecting with a church that's made up of people, many of whom you'd never choose to associate with much less be friends with. The church is made up of the same kinds of people Jesus chose to be his disciples. If you choose to get involved in a small group, it is inevitable that there is someone else in the group you wouldn't have chosen to be in the group! You know it's true and if you don't, I sure do!

Almost twenty years ago I came home from my very first seminary counselling practicum and said to my wife, "this person..." (who I then named and who to this day is a source of deep relational struggle for me, whose identity I am trying to protect!) "... is in my counselling practicum and I just know that when they assign counselling partners next week, I'm going to be paired up with this person." When the counselling pairings were announced the next week, you guessed it. I was paired up with that person! That was the one person I DIDN'T want to be paired with because of what it stirred up in me. As it turned out, I was also the last person this other individual wanted to be paired with. That's life! Doesn't God have a sense of humour?

On another occasion I was leading a small group where one of the participants was downright annoying, not just to me but to everyone in the group, including his wife! He never had a thought he didn't verbalize and some of what he verbalized bypassed the realm of thought. It was hard sometimes to be civil to him, let alone Christ-like. Maybe you've met a person like that. We had an open chair policy in our group which meant there was always room for one more person and we agreed that we would accept whoever came to fill that chair. There were times where we lived to regret our commitment to the "open chair".

Wouldn't it be nice if Jesus' "follow me" call was just an individual thing – something you could live out within the context of the trinity - me, myself, and I? Okay, maybe we'd let God into the middle of it too and make it a foursome. Or wouldn't it be easier if Jesus' "follow me" call was a call to follow with a group of people the composition of which you had some say in? What if it was a call to follow only with people you liked? It would be so much easier! It would have been so much easier for those first disciples too, but that's often not how it works with Jesus!

As I interact with people who would claim to be serious about following Jesus, perhaps one of the biggest challenges I see is that we live in a day and age where if we're willing to embrace the "follow me" call of Jesus, we want to embrace it only at an individual level. "My relationship with God is my business, not yours." We don't really have an understanding of what it means to live out that "follow me" call in the context of a community comprised of diverse, frustrating, sometimes downright annoying people not unlike that first group of disciples!

Most often what happens is that if there are enough people in a given church or small group that we don't like, we bail out on the church, the small group, the relationship, the marriage, rather than struggle through what it might mean to "follow me" the way Jesus intended it. When we bail, we do so with the illusion that we're going to find that "perfect" church, that "perfect" small group, that "perfect" relationship, that "perfect" spouse. When we find that "perfect" whatever, we're convinced it will be different. It will be better. Well I've got news for you; it's not going to happen! The one you're going to is no different than the one you just left! Whether that's a church, a small group, a relationship, a marriage partner, or a job, it's not going to be a whole lot different than the one you just left. And guess what? You take "you" with you into that "perfect" whatever! I can imagine Jesus' disciples would have liked to find that "perfect" group too!

But bailing out wasn't an option for those first twelve disciples and Jesus certainly didn't consider it an option. If anybody had legitimate reasons to bail on that group, it was Jesus. They disappointed and failed him so many times that no one would have blamed him had he chosen to find another group through whom he could bring about world change! But he didn't, not even with Judas!

Now don't get me wrong. I think there are occasionally (heavy emphasis on "occasionally") legitimate reasons to make some of those decisions, but I suspect most decisions to bail out have very little to do with having wrestled with what it means to "follow me" the way Jesus intended. We bail because we perceive it to be the better or easier option!

When Jesus was asked to identify the most important commandment, this is what he said: "'You must love the LORD your God with all your heart, all your soul, and all your mind.' This is the first and greatest commandment. A second is equally important: 'Love your neighbour as yourself.' The entire law and all the demands of the prophets are based on these two commandments." (Matthew 22:37-40) Jesus was very clear on this. The call to "follow me" means loving God and loving other people and those two cannot be separated. The Bible is clear that our love for God is manifested in our love for other people: "If someone says, 'I love God,' but hates a Christian brother or sister, that person is a liar; for if we don't love people we can see, how can we love God, whom we cannot see? And he has given us this command: Those who love God must also love their Christian brothers and sisters." (1 John 4:20-21).

The "follow me" call of Jesus is always a call to follow in the context of community, together with other people. There's no question there is an individual component to it, but there is an undeniable communal component that challenges so much of what we see reflected in our culture. In spite of all its flaws, and in the face of all its flaws, the church is still God's preferred means of incarnating His message in the world today! His plan hasn't changed! Some of the most difficult people I've encountered have helped me wrestle with Jesus' "follow me" call in my own life. Guess what? Some of those difficult relationships are more difficult today than they were when I first encountered them because today I think I have a bit better understanding of what it means to "follow me" the way Jesus intended it. I understand a bit more clearly how difficult it is to know exactly what "love" looks like lived out in those relationships. I understand a lot more clearly the price I have to pay to love some of those people. Rather than making it easier for me, my increased understanding of the "follow me" call makes it harder in those relationships!

"Follow Me" is a Call to Embrace a Lifestyle of Sacrifice

The call to "follow me" is a call to embrace a lifestyle of sacrifice. A choice to wholeheartedly embrace the "follow me" call of Jesus is going to cost you something.

A young man came to Jesus one day and asked a simple question, "What must I do to inherit eternal life?" He was a devout, religious person who had given up a lot already, but Jesus' "follow me" call stunned him; "Looking at the man, Jesus felt genuine love for him. 'There is still one thing you haven't done,' he told him. 'Go and sell all your possessions and give the money to the poor, and you will have treasure in heaven. Then come, follow me.' At this the man's face fell, and he went away sad, for he had many possessions." (Mark 10:17-31)

Jesus wasn't against money or material possessions but Jesus knew that this young man had divided allegiances and because of that he could not wholeheartedly embrace the "follow me" call. Listen to some of what Jesus has to say to those who would respond to his "follow me" call. "Whoever wants to be first must take last place and be the servant of everyone else." (Mark 10:43) "If any of you wants to be my follower, you must turn from your selfish ways, take up your cross, and follow me. If you try to hang on to your life, you will lose it. But if you give up your life for my sake and for the sake of the Good News, you will save it. And what do you benefit if you gain the whole world but lose your own soul? Is anything worth more than your soul? If anyone is ashamed of me and my message in these adulterous and sinful days, the Son of Man will be ashamed of that person when he returns in the glory of his Father with the holy angels." (Mark 8:34-38) "If you want to be my disciple, you must hate everyone else by comparison—your father and mother, wife and children, brothers and sisters—yes, even your own life. Otherwise, you cannot be my disciple. But don't begin until you count the cost." (Luke 14:26-28).

If you are willing to engage the "follow me" call of Jesus it will cost you something and it doesn't end with engaging the question once and responding. It's not like the old Fram oil filter commercial; "Pay me now or pay me later." It's, "Pay me now and pay me later!" There are always new situations that provide opportunities to wrestle with what it means to "follow me".

Whose "follow me" call has been so compelling that you have aligned your priorities in response? Are there any priorities in your life that need to be realigned? In what ways have you avoided living out that call in the context of community? Family? Church?

If the central component of what the "follow me" call looks like lived out in your life and mine is in loving God and loving others, who are the difficult people in your life whom God is calling you to love? What does it mean to love them? How can you best express love for them? Are you willing to pay the price to love them? Someone always pays a price to love! Are there sacrifices you've avoided making because you've considered the cost too high? What will you do with the two words that have changed the world? Are you willing to leave everything else behind to see those words change your world?

To respond to Jesus' "follow me" call like those twelve young men did is to experience anxiety and fear, individually and collectively. It may not look the same in each individual context but assume that the tidal wave of anxiety is rolling, and in some cases it will be a full-out tsunami! Jesus' "follow me" call is always a call to move beyond where you are now, beyond where you're comfortable. It's a call to move from the known into the unknown and that always brings with it anxiety, fear and uncertainty! Get ready for the ride but take it anyway!

For Reflection and Discussion

1. If you were to evaluate your priorities as a congregation, whose "follow me" call would you say you have responded to?

2. If you were to evaluate your individual priorities, whose "follow me" call would you say you have responded to?

3. What priorities have you radically altered in order to respond to Jesus' "follow me" call? What priorities might you need to alter in order to respond more fully? Individually? As a congregation?

4. What sacrifices have you had to make in order to respond to Jesus "follow me" call? What sacrifices might you need to make in order to respond more fully? Individually? As a congregation?

5. On a scale of 1-10 (1 being low and 10 being high), how would you say you're doing at loving God? Loving others? What steps might God be calling you to take to love him and others more completely? Individually? As a congregation?

6. On a scale of 1-10 (1 being low and 10 being high), how would you rate your experience of meaningful, authentic spiritual community as a congregation? Why do you think that is? What could you do to increase your collective response to Jesus' "follow me" call related to community?

Chapter 4
Grenwich - "Following Who?"

Five months after their initial visit, Barry, Diane, and their kids arrived at Grenwich to lots of excitement and enthusiasm. Equally excited, Barry hit the ministry ground running. He quickly discovered that he enjoyed the opportunity to preach on a weekly basis and people seemed to respond well to it. Before long, Sunday morning worship attendance began to swell, necessitating the set-up of additional chairs. Within a few short months attendance had broken the 100 barrier as new people from the community (mostly from other churches) began attending and calling Grenwich "home".

David and the other leaders were excited about the influx of new people. It gave them status in the community and Barry was quickly learning that status was an important metric at Grenwich. He had come to realize that was one of the reasons they called him to be their pastor. He had a leadership role within the denomination, the prominence of which was valued at Grenwich. His decision to accept the call to Grenwich was considered by David Hill to have been somewhat of a coup.

Barry, on the other hand, wasn't nearly as enamoured by the growth. He knew that many of these new people had left previous churches with unresolved "baggage"; they had left disillusioned, disgruntled, unhappy. Most had not processed their leaving well and Barry was afraid that it was only a matter of time before he or someone at Grenwich did something that would upset them, in the process activating the proverbial "revolving door", a permanent fixture in virtually every church. He knew that Grenwich was no different than any other church, however, he wanted to do his part to see rust develop on the hinge plate of that revolving door! He did his best to inform those coming to Grenwich that it wasn't a perfect church, and he wasn't a perfect pastor. As much as people indicated they knew that to be true, Barry wasn't convinced.

In spite of the fact that this was the first church where Barry had overall leadership responsibility for the entire congregation, he had come to Grenwich recognizing the importance of rallying the congregation around a common vision and mission. So he began to focus the Grenwich leadership on their stated vision, mission, and goals document. He somewhat naively believed that because this document had been approved by the congregation there wouldn't be any resistance to actually using it as a template and compass to guide their collective leadership and ministry efforts. He would soon find out that he was misguided in his assumption.

The more that Barry focused on Grenwich's stated vision, mission and goals the more people from the community showed up for a visit at Sunday morning worship services. And as more people from the community showed up at Sunday morning worship services, the more word spread in the community about what was happening at Grenwich. Equally significant was that more of those who visited chose Grenwich to be the place where they would find community and explore faith and ministry.

Within 18 months of Barry commencing ministry, average attendance had ballooned to 150, double what it was when he started. While things were positive and upbeat, the waters were stirring deep beneath the surface. Not everything was as upbeat as it appeared on the surface at Grenwich! The waves of anxiety and fear were starting to ripple their way through the subterranean recesses of church life. Long established members of Grenwich no longer knew everyone who was a part of the congregation; there were so many strange faces. The comfort level they had been so familiar with was being stretched and there were a host of unknowns. Uncertainty was something to be feared. Change was something to be resisted. Predictability and familiarity needed to be preserved and restored!

While the growth was exciting at one level, at other levels it was putting pressure on an infrastructure that wasn't designed to handle the rapidity of the growth. The thirty-something year old facility was quickly being taxed, not only in terms of worship space, but support space as well. While the designated sanctuary space could accommodate 150 (pushing beyond the generally accepted 80% capacity ratio before growth was stifled) the foyer was designed to handle 100 at most, and the Children's Ministry space was designed to accommodate 30 to 40, so the space challenges were accentuated and quickly becoming acute.

The growth had prompted discussions of building expansion and as such a Building Committee had been put in place to begin exploring the options. Comprised of quality, gifted people, some relative "newcomers" had also been included on the committee. They brought fresh and different perspectives than those held by long term members of Grenwich, in particular David Hill. While many would have seen this as a positive development, this would prove to become problematic as the balance of power began to shift in this growing congregation. Not surprisingly, the level of latent anxiety and fear began to escalate. People like David were afraid their hold on power and their ability to influence the direction of the church was slipping away and with it a significant piece of their personal identity within the church. Who they were as people was tied up in the sphere and scope of their influence in the church.

As the Building Committee began their work, parallel albeit informal discussions were taking place as to how the congregation might finance such an expansion. One of those discussions took place in Barry's office and involved David Hill. David dropped by Barry's office one day and the conversation quickly shifted to the Building Committee's work. David indicated that he had a piece of property which he had sold, the final payment of which was coming due shortly. He indicated that he would be willing to commit that payment, a sizeable six-figure amount representing approximately 15% of the projected cost of facility expansion, towards the building fund. Trying to hide his excitement at what this might mean for the facility expansion moving forward, Barry affirmed David's generosity. There was no denying this was a significant conversation and a significant amount of money. What Barry didn't realize was how significant that conversation would turn out to be, and in a way he certainly didn't expect!

As the Building Committee continued their work, they left no stone unturned in the due diligence process, exploring a host of facility expansion options. One of their challenges had to do with the original design of the building. While it had incorporated future expansion to accommodate a new, larger sanctuary, there was no provision for additional foyer, office, or ministry space. The Building Committee realized that a pursuit of the original expansion plans would be short-sighted at best, and at worst irresponsible stewardship of the congregation's financial resources.

As a result, they began to explore alternative plans that would expand the facility to the east, utilizing some of the existing parking lot. The plans that emerged from those discussions generated excitement and momentum among committee members, in part because this option would address foyer, office, and ministry space needs as well as increase worship capacity. As word trickled out to others outside of the committee, the excitement was shared by many. But not by all.

A few committee members showed up at the church parking lot one spring evening with measuring tape and stakes in hand. They carefully measured out the proposed building expansion, driving a stake at the corners of what might become the new building. David Hill just "happened" to drive by the church that evening, saw the "commotion" and decided to see what was going on. Not a member of the committee, but a long term member of the church who had an incredible amount of historical influence, he considered any church business his business and this was no exception. What he found out that night was not to his liking! Never shy about expressing his opinion David voiced his disapproval of the plan in his usual, forceful style. The committee members present challenged him, which was an unfamiliar experience for David. These individuals had no ties to him or to the long term history of the church and as such weren't intimidated by his influence and position on this or any other issue.

David had been a member of the Grenwich congregation for over forty years, many of those in key leadership positions. Urban legend had it that the church constitution had been amended in order to facilitate his removal from his position as chair of the Church Board, a position he had held for fifteen consecutive years. Barry believed it to be more than legend – he believed it to be the way things really happened! Both that David had been the chair of the church Board for fifteen consecutive years, and that the church would not deal with the issue in an up-front kind of manner, but would rather skirt around it to arrive at the same outcome.

David operated with a sense of entitlement when it came to matters of the church. When the church couldn't afford to pay its bills, David increased his giving to the church so that the church had the required funds to pay the bills. Or he paid them out of his personal bank account! As such, he felt he had a right to have his say, and his way. And his say should be THE way! It was never discussed at a congregational meeting. It was never brought up at a church Board meeting. It was just the way it was and everyone who had any history in the church knew it to be true, accepting it as "gospel." The occasional soul would dare utter an under the breath complaint, but rarely would it reach the level where a general audience could make sense of the complaint. Everyone knew that David was going to do what David was going to do, never out in the open at a formal meeting though. He would quietly work the crowd behind the scenes, garnering the support he deemed necessary so that when a decision needed to be formally made, the outcome was a fait accompli. David's allies would vote his way and the decision would proceed. While the process appeared on the surface to be democratic, the result of a "free" vote, it was far from democratic and far from "free." There were always strings attached!

The decision to force the issue of David's tenure in leadership through a constitutional change said as much about the systemic pattern of the church as it did about David. It revealed a latent fear in the congregation. A fear of engaging the conflict they knew would erupt should anyone suggest that David step aside; a fear of David's reaction and the potential loss of his financial support for the church, something which most people knew was significant. So rather than name their fear and address the deeper issues, they took the path of least resistance and changed the constitution. While they didn't realize it, the process served to keep their anxiety at bay, although anxiety and fear were the primary motivators behind their chosen course of action.

With the church growing as it was, David's influence was gradually being diluted and his voice muted. Some of those new to the church were not afraid to voice opinions contrary to David's opinions. They weren't afraid to challenge his opinions. Because these people had formalized their relationship with Grenwich through church membership (and more important by generously supporting the ministries of the church financially), a value dear to David's heart, they now had equal opportunity (at least according to the church constitution) to speak and vote on matters of importance to the life of the church. In David's mind, however, not everyone was equal. In his mind, his voted trumped any other vote or any combination of votes. While he never stated it that way, it was clearly his underlying belief.

In the week following the encounter in the parking lot with members of the Building Committee, David dropped by Barry's office. The conversation started off as it normally did, superficial and congenial, but it quickly turned to more serious matters. Having seen the stakes in the parking lot, Barry was unaware of David's parking lot encounter but he was quickly apprised of the specifics, at least David's version of them. Barry was unprepared for what was about to come out of David's mouth. "I'm not sure that I can contribute to the building if the proposed expansion to the east goes ahead," David offered. Barry couldn't believe what he was hearing!

He had been around enough to know that David was threatening to withdraw his sizeable, stated financial commitment to the building. For some reason, Barry knew David was completely serious! He meant what he was saying! Barry also knew that David expected him to cave in to his demands!

Barry took a moment to collect his thoughts reflecting on one of David's favourite mantras, "We have a congregational form of church government here! The congregation makes the final decision!" David usually offered those comments when he felt that some individual or group were threatening to wield too much power in a direction he didn't agree with. Never had that phrase been turned back on David when he took similar action, at least not as far as Barry knew. He began to wonder how David's comments fit with one of his own oft repeated "values". Barry could feel his heart starting to beat a bit faster. He knew he had to challenge what David had just said to him, but he was afraid. He wasn't sure how David would respond because he'd never found himself in this exact position before. He knew he couldn't let David's comment go unaddressed. It was blackmail and it needed to be addressed.

In spite of his fears, Barry calmly but firmly reminded David of his "value". "David, we have a congregational form of church government here. You and I each have an opportunity to state our opinion at congregational meetings, but at the end of the day, it's the congregation's decision to make. The church constitution stipulates quite clearly that the majority rules on matters such as this. If the congregation decides an expansion to the east is the way God is calling us to go, I would hope that you would continue to support the building to the same degree you have already indicated you would." The conversation ended abruptly with David leaving the office. Little did Barry realize the importance of what had just transpired and what the implications might be. But he was soon to find out. He didn't fully appreciate how much he had disrupted the proverbial apple cart in a way that would very quickly bring the latent anxiety within the congregation to the surface in a way that it could no longer be ignored!

For Reflection and Discussion

1. What thoughts or feelings get stirred up as you reflect on this part of the story at Grenwich? In what ways can you relate? Individually? As a congregation?

2. What thoughts or feelings do you have towards Barry Moffat? David Hill? How do you think you would have responded had you been in Barry's situation?

3. As you reflect on the life of your congregation, where have you seen similar patterns to those experienced at Grenwich?

4. Assuming that every congregation has at least one person like David Hill, how has your church historically chosen to deal with those kind of people and situations? Is there one situation in particular that stands out? What were the specifics of that situation? How do you see fear and anxiety at work in that situation?

5. Can you identify situations where you or your congregation have made decisions motivated by anxiety and fear? What was the situation and the decision? Looking back, what could you have done differently?

Ken Thiessen

Chapter 5
Measuring What Matters - To Jesus

I'm sure you've never encountered a church like Grenwich; never encountered an individual like David Hill. I say that somewhat tongue in cheek. Sad to say, there are many churches like Grenwich and many individuals like David Hill. What is somewhat unusual is encountering a pastor like Barry Moffat, someone prepared to challenge the underlying dynamics in order to give the church the opportunity to learn new and more biblical ways of relating and making decisions, more biblical expressions of what it means to be "community". What you may not have considered is that anxiety is the common thread throughout, even if it doesn't appear so to the naked eye.

Every church measures something. Grenwich did. David Hill did. Barry Moffat did. You do. Your pastor does. Your church does. It happens in many of the institutions which make up the fabric of our society. Metrics and measurement are ingrained in so many aspects of our lives that oftentimes we're not even aware that we're being measured, or that we're measuring others. The things we measure serve as a window into the systemic anxiety that's present.

The education system is just one example. Teachers engage the arduous process of trying to impart important information to students in a way that will forever transform their lives and equip them to be responsible citizens. They measure the effectiveness of the learning process by grading those students on various assignment and exams and the results are reflected in a report card. Those report cards help calm some students' anxiety and heighten anxiety for others depending on their interpretation of the grades received.

Ironically report cards are anxiety inducing for the teacher as well. If the whole class does well, the natural conclusion is that the teacher has done well, easing her anxiety. If the class does poorly, it may be a sign that the teacher has not been as effective in communicating the course material in a way that was understood by the students. That outcome is anxiety-inducing for the teacher.

We live in a world that constantly measures things and people. But it begs the question: what's the standard of measurement and what kinds of tools do you use to measure? My decision to follow God's call into ministry meant I had to break a vow made many years earlier; a vow to never, ever enter the doors of higher learning for any other purpose than a visit! So off I went to Bible College and Seminary. There I discovered that different professors used different approaches to "measure" my learning. My Systematic Theology professor measured me in large part on the basis of whether or not I could accurately fill in the blanks and regurgitate the notes and handouts we had been given in class. My History professor asked me to outline the significant factors and events which contributed to the Protestant Reformation. Both professors were measuring me as a student; one was measuring my ability to memorize and recall specific words and phrases and the other was measuring my ability to integrate the major events and themes which had shaped a particular period of history. Some of us were deemed to "pass" and some of us were deemed to "fail" on the basis of our ability to meet the measurement standard applied.

We live in a world that constantly measures things and people. You can't get in a car and leave your driveway without being reminded of different types of measurements. The amount of fuel in the fuel tank, the temperature of the engine, the oil pressure, the speed of the car; the list could go on and on. Daily we are reminded of the value of our investments in the latest stock market updates. The value of the currency which enables us to purchase goods in our communities is constantly measured in relationship to other world currencies. The more fluctuation there is in the value of our investment portfolios or the value of our currency of trade, the greater the degree of systemic angst across the country. We live in a world that constantly measures things and people.

We measure people by the colour of their skin, their competency with the English language, the neighbourhoods and homes they live in, the cars they drive, where they work, the clothes they wear, the social habits they choose to participate in or not participate in, their political beliefs, their sports allegiances, their community status. It happens in society and it happens in the church.

I grew up in a church community where I intuitively knew to question the spirituality of anyone who attended a church from a different denomination and the basis of my measurement was the fact that many of them drank beer after church league slow-pitch baseball games and exited church services to light up a cigarette. According to my measurement standards, how could anyone drink beer, smoke cigarettes and call themselves a Christian? I grew up to intuitively measure them as people who just went through the motions of their religious experience, participated in the rituals of their particular faith community and then went out unchanged to live life as they did before. I intuitively knew they weren't going to be in heaven with "us". I grew up measuring those whose pattern and practise of worship was different than mine, sometimes even labelling them as a "cult".

I grew up being told on more than one occasion that going to a movie theatre was wrong and un-Christian. I grew up not having a television in our home until I was 10 years old. Occasionally we would rent one for the National Hockey League Stanley Cup playoffs but it would be returned as soon as the playoffs were done. I grew up being reprimanded for purchasing Simon and Garfunkel's "Bridge Over Troubled Water" album - an actual vinyl record, not a CD or a download from iTunes!

I grew up in a culture where our youth pastor was measured and reprimanded by quite a large segment of people in the church because he wore a coloured dress shirt to church on a Sunday. It didn't matter that he was wearing a sports jacket, dress pants, AND a tie, his shirt wasn't white. I grew up in a culture where it was perfectly acceptable for a woman to plant a church and provide pastoral leadership in Africa but could not preach in our church in North America, she could only "share" her testimony.

I grew up in a culture where I learned to measure what was right, what was wrong, people who were right, people who were wrong. I don't ever recall hearing many sermons to that effect, but it was something I just knew to be "true". The measurement standards served to help control the systemic anxiety. We didn't have to wonder what was "right" and what was "wrong", who was "in" or who was "out". The collective measurement standard helped keep the systemic anxiety in check.

What a shock when I accepted the call of a particular church in my first formal pastoral staff position, only to discover well stocked liquor cabinets in the homes of all the key leaders. These were people whose cultural background was very different than mine as were their measurement standards! As I got to know them, I realized that many of them were deeply committed to serving the same God I was.

What a shock when I moved to another community where the largest churches were some of the same churches that I had grown to question and label as "unchristian" or a "cult" because of some of their social practises and worship patterns. You can imagine the kind of theological gymnastics I had to go through as I fellowshipped together with the pastors of these respective congregations in the local gathering of pastors. What an eye-opener to discover that these were people who also loved the same God I did, and sometimes loved him more and better than I did!

We live in a world that constantly measures things and people. I am prone to measure things and people but I have also been subjected to other people's measurement standards. You know that by virtue of your own experience as well.

But who determines what gets measured? Is it you? Me? The person with the most money? The person who has been in the church the longest? The person with the most education or the most theological education? The person who can debate and argue the best? Who determines what gets measured?

I can imagine that some of you may feel sorry for me as you reflect on my experiences. Because you were measured by different standards, you consider that I've been raised in a repressive kind of environment. I didn't experience it as overly repressive; it was all I knew. It was "normal". I can also imagine that some might think I have abandoned the essentials of the Christian faith because you use a different measurement standard.

The Anxious Congregation

Who determines what's going to be the measurement standard? What if we've been measuring the wrong things well, or measuring the right things poorly, or not at all? A review of the book of Ecclesiastes reminds us that there is nothing new under the sun. We are not the first generation to experience this. Jesus faced this issue with great regularity and he spoke into those situations with great passion, conviction, and emphasis.

One such situation is recorded in Matthew's Gospel where we find Jesus engaged in a highly charged discourse with the religious leaders and Pharisees. They had their PhD. in Measurement, priding themselves on their ability to accurately measure things and people. There was only one small problem; Jesus was unimpressed! Notice what he says: "What sorrow awaits you teachers of religious law and you Pharisees. Hypocrites! For you are careful to tithe even the tiniest income from your herb gardens, but you ignore the more important aspects of the law—justice, mercy, and faith. You should tithe, yes, but do not neglect the more important things. Blind guides! You strain your water so you won't accidentally swallow a gnat, but you swallow a camel! What sorrow awaits you teachers of religious law and you Pharisees. Hypocrites! For you are so careful to clean the outside of the cup and the dish, but inside you are filthy—full of greed and self-indulgence! You blind Pharisee! First wash the inside of the cup and the dish, and then the outside will become clean, too. What sorrow awaits you teachers of religious law and you Pharisees. Hypocrites! For you are like whitewashed tombs—beautiful on the outside but filled on the inside with dead people's bones and all sorts of impurity. Outwardly you look like righteous people, but inwardly your hearts are filled with hypocrisy and lawlessness." (Matthew 23:23-28)

It doesn't take a rocket scientist to discern Jesus' sentiments! He's quite a bit less than impressed!

What Did the Pharisees Measure?

What did the Pharisees measure and what was it about what they measured that so upset Jesus?

They measured the external appearance of spirituality. Jesus said, "Everything they do is for show." (Matthew 23:5) It was about wearing the right clothes, hanging out with the right people, and being addressed with the proper title. It was about washing the outside of the cup which people could see and ignoring the inside of the cup which people couldn't see. That's what they measured. That's how they expected to be measured.

They measured the approval of men. It was important that they were addressed using the right title and paid the honour due their title and their role. They measured their diligence in seeking converts, "For you cross land and sea to make one convert." They were serious about going out and inviting others to join them on the way, willing to pay a significant price. They were always trying to get more "bums in the pews" for Sabbath services and did they ever feel good when they succeeded!

They measured and prided themselves on their observance of the minutia of the law. Jesus said, "You tithe even the tiniest income from your herb gardens - mint, dill, and cumin." Old Testament Law required that a Jewish person give 10% or a tithe of their income as an offering to God. The Pharisees took this so far as to obsessively weigh out precisely 10% of their dill and cumin seed, and their mint. I don't know but about you, but I'd suggest this was the earliest form of obsessive compulsive disorder! Have you ever tried to measure out precisely 10% of a jar of dill seed?

The Pharisees then took their emphasis on metrics and measurement and spiritualized it making it a spiritual virtue, not realizing that it was a sign of serious spiritual dysfunction! Then they applied that same measure to everyone else. You were deemed to be a "failure" if you didn't observe and hold to the same measurement standard in each of these areas.

What Didn't the Pharisees Measure?

What didn't the Pharisees measure? One of the key things Jesus challenged them on was their failure to measure the motivations of their heart. Were they humble servants or arrogant and harsh task masters? Were their actions motivated by a love for God and for people, which was at the heart of following God, or was it all about them? If they had measured this then Jesus would not have described them saying, "They crush people with unbearable religious demands and never lift a finger to ease the burden."

But there was a second thing that Jesus challenged them on. They failed to measure whether or not they had God's approval. They were so consumed with the approval of man that God's approval didn't even dot their radar screen. They failed to measure whether or not their methods actually moved people closer to the kingdom or further from it. If they had measured this then Jesus would not have rebuked them saying, "For you shut the door of the Kingdom of Heaven in people's faces. You won't go in yourselves, and you don't let others enter either."

They also failed to measure whether their evangelism was making true disciples or just another stat for the record book. If they had measured this then Jesus wouldn't have characterized their evangelistic zeal this way, "For you cross land and sea to make one convert, and then you turn that person into twice the child of hell you yourselves are!" Can you imagine hearing that if you were one of the Pharisees?

But there's another challenge Jesus raised. They failed to measure whether or not they were also keeping the major points of the law such as justice (treating people fairly, doing what is right), mercy (showing compassion and kindness to the poor and miserable), faithfulness to God. If they had, Jesus wouldn't have said to them, "You ignore the more important aspects of the law—justice, mercy, and faith."

The final thing that I want to draw attention to is that they failed to measure the level of their own self-deception. They were completely unaware of how far off the mark they were! If they had measured this, Jesus wouldn't have said to them, "Inside you are filthy, full of greed and self-indulgence! Outwardly you look like righteous people, but inwardly your hearts are filled with hypocrisy and lawlessness. You are like whitewashed tombs - beautiful on the outside but filled on the inside with dead people's bones and all sorts of impurity."

What Do We Measure?

Now we're not like that at all in the 21st Century. Maybe in those "other" churches. Maybe those "legalists." But certainly not you or me! Certainly not your church! You never count bums in the pew do you? You would never think of measuring the size of the weekly offering! You don't measure people based on external appearances of spirituality do you? You don't measure yourselves that way do you? Sure they did that in the Bible times. Saul was chosen to be king because he looked good; he was tall, dark, and handsome. When Samuel was called to pick a king out of Jesse's family, David was the last one he'd have picked, but he was God's first choice. God saw something much deeper than what Samuel saw.

Let's be honest. We're more guilty than we care to admit! And more anxious! Most of us walk in the door of any given church on any given Sunday and we know the routine. We put on our Sunday smile and we feel as if we have to look right, dress right, say the right thing, have our act together. You feel it and if you don't, I do. At least one couple in any given church on any given Sunday (or whatever day you gather for corporate worship) had a fight before they left for church. They walk in the door and they're "fine". At least one family in any given church on any given Sunday had kids that were less than cooperative and left the house upset. But by the time they arrive at church, they're "fine". You wear the right clothes and have the smile pasted on and people assume you're "fine".

I know that because I lived it obsessively for years and it worked. People thought I had my spiritual act together and left me alone. I'm not as bad, but I still live that way more than I would like. More than one prominent church leader has dressed the part, played the part, fooled people into thinking that everything was "fine" all the while living a life that was crashing in around them. How would you measure me if I had body piercings, tattoos, wore shorts and a t-shirt. Not very appropriate for a pastor let alone someone who might be in position of denominational leadership or doing consulting work with your church. At least in some contexts! Says who? I wonder if Jesus ever wore a suit or a tie? Do you think that's what mattered most to him?

Now don't hear me saying that we shouldn't measure things. That's not what Jesus was saying! But do we measure what matters? What do you measure in your personal life? Do you measure externals or do you measure what matters?

Do you measure how your heart is doing? Do you measure your love for God and for other people? Do you have places where your self-deception can be exposed in a loving way that moves you closer to the kingdom? Do you measure not only your observance of the minutia of the law but also the major points of the law, like loving God, loving people, justice, mercy and faithfulness. The measure you use for yourself will most likely be the measure you use with other people.

How do you measure yourself as a church? One of the primary measurements that is used to evaluate any staff person in a church is how many people show up and attend. Whether that is for Sunday morning worship, small groups, youth, young adults, or children's ministry, the greater the numbers the more "successful" the staff person is deemed to be. Other metrics are the size of the weekly offering, or the number of people on the membership roll, or the size of the church campus. The list could go on and on. Numbers are one measurement indicator but are they an important indicator or even the most important?

If Jesus was more concerned with the heart than the externals, might it not be more prudent to measure the reason why people come, or measure the outcome of their attendance. Is their attendance at a particular function, event or program in some way moving them to love God and other people more deeply? If not, do the numbers really matter? What really matters when it comes to measuring worship services? Is it about how many people left feeling good? Is it about how many choruses were sung and how many hymns were sung? I recently attended a church service and I said to the minister afterwards, "I didn't enjoy your sermon, but you were faithful to the text!" We had a good chuckle and then talked about how the truth of Scripture when preached faithfully, sometimes doesn't feel good! So if one of my metrics is leaving church feeling good, then that minister got an "F". But if the more accurate (and more important) metric is the faithful exposition of the text, he got an "A+".

In one church I served I was responsible for selecting music for Sunday services and for a whole year I tracked every song we sang. We sang 51% choruses and 49% hymns and it still wasn't good enough. Nobody was happy! Is it about bums in the pew, the size of the offering, the number of people involved in various leadership roles? Or is it perhaps about something more than that? Might we get a more accurate measurement by asking deeper questions?

For leaders and those planning services, might these be better questions to ask: Did our efforts to plan and lead worship this morning invite people to more deeply understand God's love for them and his call on their lives and then desire to live out that call more fully for this upcoming week? Did I prepare my own heart to lead and was I open to what God wanted to do in me even as I prepared to lead?

For participants, might these be better questions to ask: Did I come prepared to offer God something of myself today? Was I open to what he wanted to say to me through every aspect of the service whether it met my preferences or not? Was I willing to respond to whatever it was that he called me to as I left this service?

There have been Sundays where the pastor could have danced on the head of a pin, the music team and musicians could have rocked the house, and individuals wouldn't have been impressed or moved in their spirit and it would have had nothing to do with the leaders up front. It would have had everything to do with the individual. Those kind of questions cut more to the heart of the matter and call us to measure what matters. But they also raise the anxiety level because they call us to live in the unknown. How do we really KNOW how we're doing if we focus on the qualitative measurements proposed by Jesus rather than the quantitative measurements imposed by the Pharisees?

When Measuring What Matters Matters!

I learned a very valuable lesson about why measuring what matters really matters on an airplane flight. We were in our final approach for landing when the pilot informed us the landing might be a bit rough due to the residual effects of thunderstorms in the area. Surprisingly the landing was relatively smooth and uneventful until we were about 30 feet above the runway! Just when you would expect the engine noise to subside, they roared to life and instead of landing we were on a steep incline away from the runway. Travelling with a friend, we had been "blessed" to have a large class of junior high students board our plane, returning from a school field trip. They were normal, energetic and boisterous teenagers who had disrupted what we had hoped would be a quiet ride home. When the plane began to quickly ascend, these junior high students were less than calm, panicked in fact, and even seasoned travellers were grabbing the "lunch" bag in the seat pocket in front of them. We ascended away from the airport heading off to the south east and after what seemed like an eternity the pilot apologetically explained what had happened. Due to the residual effects in the wake of the thunderstorm, the instrument panel on the Boeing 737 flashed a wind shear warning. Since airline safety is of utmost importance, he indicated he would try landing from another direction.

Wikipedia describes a wind shear as a difference in wind speed and/or direction over a relatively short distance in the atmosphere. It has particularly drastic affects on aircraft that are either in the final stages of landing or the initial stages of take off, often resulting in a crash and certain loss of life. In 1988 the U.S. Federal Aviation Administration mandated that all commercial aircraft have on-board wind shear detection systems by 1993. The result of these efforts was immediate. Between 1964 and 1985, wind shear directly caused or contributed to 26 major civil transport aircraft accidents in the U.S. that led to 620 deaths and 200 injuries. Since 1995, the number of major civil aircraft accidents caused by wind shear has dropped to approximately one every ten years. Talk about the importance of measuring what matters!

What if aircraft instrumentation measured everything but wind shear? History bears out the catastrophic consequences. There's a parallel to personal and church life. When we measure everything but spiritual "wind shear", the results are catastrophic. If we don't measure what matters personally, the results are catastrophic and there are casualties. If we don't measure what matters corporately as churches, the results are equally catastrophic. There are casualties.

What are you measuring personally? What are you measuring corporately as a church? Are you measuring what matters? Personally I'd rather measure the right things poorly than measure the wrong things well and live in the anxiety of that process!

In his book, The Unquenchable Worshiper, Matt Redman, song-writer and worship pastor shares the story behind his song, *The Heart of Worship*.[4] Matt was informed by his Senior Pastor that there would be no more music during morning worship until a song emerged spontaneously from the people. The pastor sensed that their worship had become vain repetition and ritual. Matt shares the devastating impact of this news. You see, he measured himself by his ability to lead

---

[4] Matt Redman, The Unquenchable Worshipper. Coming Back to the Heart of Worship. (Ventura, CA: Regal Books, 2001), 102-104

the congregation in worship. Who was he if he wasn't a worship leader? But during that time, God gave him the song, *The Heart of Worship*.

When the music fades
All is stripped away
And I simply come
Longing just to bring
Something that's of worth
That will bless Your heart

I bring You more than a song
For a song in itself
Is not what You have required
You search much deeper within
Through the way things appear
You're looking into my heart

I'm coming back to the heart of worship
And it's all about You
It's all about You, Jesus
I'm sorry Lord for the thing I've made it
When it's all about You
It's all about You, Jesus

King of endless worth
No one could express
How much You deserve
Though I'm weak and poor
All I have is Yours
Every single breath

God taught Matt something about measuring what matters. I suspect your congregation is probably not unlike the church Matt was a part of. There are probably aspects of your life that have become vain repetition and ritual. What do you measure personally? What does your congregation measure? Are you measuring what matters to Jesus?

For Reflection and Discussion

1. What's your reaction to Ken's experience of the metrics he grew up with? What's your experience related to metrics? In what ways is it similar/different to Ken's experience? How does your church compare with the church Ken grew up in as it relates to metrics and measuring what matters?

2. What do you measure in your personal life? How have you arrived at those metrics?

3. What do you measure as a church? How have you arrived at those metrics? Are there things you should be measuring and aren't? If so, what are they? Are there things you are measuring that you should stop measuring? If so, how would you decide what to stop measuring?

4. How do you respond to the statement: "I'd rather measure the right things poorly than measure the wrongs things well"? Where do you think your church fits in relationship to this statement?

5. How do you measure the level of your self-deception? Individually? As a church? What checks and balances do you have in place to ensure you're not fooling yourself, individually or as a church?

Ken Thiessen

Chapter 6
Grenwich - What We Measure "Matters"!

Unbeknownst to Barry, in that fateful meeting with David he had broken one of the cardinal rules in the game of long term pastoral tenure at Grenwich, namely "Stand up to David Hill at your own peril!" The trouble was, few had ever risked addressing their own anxiety and facing their own fears to see what would happen should they step outside the parameters they all knew as "normal". Barry was soon to find out, because from that day on, David's attitude and posture towards Barry changed.

Where David had been one of the strongest proponents and supporters of Barry's hiring, he now began to work behind the scenes, lobbying for Barry's removal as lead pastor. It didn't matter what the issue was, David found a way to draw a straight line connection back to Barry. Fuelling his efforts was his fear that his influence in the congregation was diminishing even further. On the other hand, Barry's vision and leadership was gaining momentum and influence, and David was afraid that he was quickly losing his grip on the rudder which had set the church's direction for so many years. The decision years earlier to change the constitution limiting his tenure as board chair, the approval of the vision and goals document, calling Barry as Senior Pastor, and now the rapid growth in the church had all served to undermine his historic grip on power.

What David didn't realize was that his own anxiety level had spiked. The only way he knew how to manage it was to redirect that anxiety somewhere else, and at someone else, and make them the scapegoat! He had to redouble his efforts to remove the one person whom he saw as responsible in the present, the person who most represented a threat to his continued influence and control. That person was Barry Moffat.

While David was working his "magic" behind the scenes, on the surface things continued to unfold according to plan. Or so it seemed. Ministry was going well, the church continued to experience growth, and the building expansion discussions were proceeding. So well in fact that the Building Committee was prepared to bring a presentation to the congregation along with a recommendation as to the preferred course of action. They were hoping the congregation would agree to conduct a vote and proceed in accordance with the outcome of the vote. Their recommendation suggested that the congregation in fact move forward with a facility expansion to the east, in direct opposition to what David wanted to see happen. As the congregation met to discuss the recommendation of the Building Committee, there was good, open dialogue and deliberation. A motion was made (by a relatively new member of the congregation) that an 80% affirmative vote be the threshold for moving forward. That motion was seconded, discussed and passed by an overwhelming majority. It was decided that the vote would take place over the next several weeks so as to give as many as possible an opportunity to participate in the democratic process, particularly given the importance of the decision. It was also agreed that while only the votes of members would determine the final outcome, committed adherents (many of whom would help cover the costs of facility expansion) would also be encouraged to register their "vote" so as to give leadership a clearer understanding of the broader level of support for the project. Those most invested in the expansion quietly questioned the wisdom of the 80% threshold, Barry included, but there was a sense that if God was in this, whatever the outcome, it would be right for the congregation.

When the "polls" closed and the votes were tallied, member support totalled 72%, 8 percentage points short of the required 80% threshold! Many of the 72% were bewildered, confused, and disillusioned. "Whose bright idea was that 80% anyway? 72% is an overwhelming majority! We should proceed anyway!" Ironically, one of the chief proponents of this sentiment and advocates for this direction was David Hill! As much as Barry was confused and bewildered like the rest, he believed that somewhere in this decision God was at work. Not sure how, he cautioned David against a unilateral and arbitrary disregard for the will of the people as they had responded to what they felt was the leading of God. The congregation had been clear in affirming the 80% threshold, so any action by leadership contrary to that would undermine their credibility in the eyes of the congregation.

David was undeterred, intensifying his efforts to gain support for Barry's removal as Lead Pastor of the church. Attending a denominational gathering, David arranged to meet with the District Superintendent, the denominational leader responsible for pastoral placement, to discuss the "need" for new pastoral leadership at Grenwich. Unbeknownst to David, Barry observed their meeting, and intuitively knew the subject matter of their discussions. Within days, Barry received a call from the District Superintendent who informed Barry that "David Hill is not one of your strongest supporters. He thinks you're a good pastor, but that you'd be better suited for another church." Barry was neither surprised nor shocked.

With a Board meeting on the horizon, and aware that he would be meeting with David as Board Chair to formulate the agenda, Barry knew he needed to raise the issue with David. Just the thought of that caused Barry's heart to race. With each confrontation with David, the stakes were raised, the risks more pronounced. Barry's anxiety level increased, fuelled by his fear of what David's next course of action might be. If David was successful in removing Barry from his position as Lead Pastor, how would Barry provide for his family? How would he deal with the emotional trauma of that? Which church would consider him to be their pastor if he had an unceremonious exit from Grenwich? Questions with no answers! Questions which triggered deep seated fears. In the face of his fears, and in spite of his fears, he was wrestling with what it meant to love God, love David Hill, love the church and do what was right. How could he discern what really was the right thing to do?

Sure enough, David dropped by Barry's office a day or two later to talk about the agenda for the upcoming Board meeting. David was his usual friendly self, giving no indication that anything was awry or betraying his real feelings about Barry. That was consistent with David's pattern. Barry's heart was pounding because he knew this was all a charade. The pleasantries dispensed with, Barry decided to face his fears, move beyond his anxiety and he spoke into the open what had been taking place behind the scenes. "I understand you had a meeting with Larry Harding." David's face instantly turned an ashen grey. Without missing a beat he said, "Barry, I think you'd make a great District Superintendent. I've been really disappointed with the people the denomination has appointed as District Superintendents. I think you'd make a great one!"

"Well David," Barry replied, "what are you saying about my ministry here?"

"I think it's done and I think you should just quietly go away! I don't think you can salvage it."

Barry could hardly believe what he was hearing! His anxiety level sky-rocketed as he tried to come to terms with the words that had just come out of David's mouth. Had he made a huge mistake? Should he have given in to his fears and kept his mouth shut? So many of the signs were positive, Sure the vote had fallen just short of the 80% threshold, but that didn't discount the genuine working of God in the ministry and life of Grenwich Community Church!

"So you really believe that if I quietly resign people in the church aren't going to suspect something more sinister? You really think they'll buy it, especially if I don't have anywhere else to go?"

"I think so," David replied. "In fact, I think you're going to have a hard time getting people to let their names stand for leadership when the Nominating Committee starts contacting people here shortly. People are going to refuse to get involved because of you."

"Really! You think that if I resign the Nominating Committee's job is going to be easier?"

"I do!" David said.

"Are you willing to take the risk?" Barry queried?

"I think so" was the reply. Barry was dumbfounded at the audacity and the depth of what he perceived to be self-deception on David's part. What he didn't question was the depth of David's convictions, or his ongoing resolve to do something about it!

"David, if there's a problem with my leadership, we have a process for addressing that as a church. The Constitution is clear about what that process is. Why don't we bring it up at the Board meeting and talk about it. If there's a problem, I'm more than open to deal with it."

"I'm afraid someone's going to call for a vote of confidence," was the return response.

"I'm fine with that," Barry offered. "If I don't have the confidence of the people, I'll respect that, but if I do have the confidence of the people, then you respect that."

"I think that's the worst thing we could do," David shot back.

"No, David. What you've been doing for the last three months going around behind the scenes has been far worse," Barry replied somewhat painfully. "Why don't we bring in the District Superintendent? Part of his role is to help churches and pastors deal with these kinds of situations."

David was unrelenting. "No, the District Superintendent can't help us. He has nothing to offer. I think you should just resign." And with that he left Barry's office.

Barry sat silent for what seemed like an eternity. He could not believe what had just happened. Seminary had never prepared him for an encounter the likes of which he had just experienced. Little did he know what yet awaited him! Never had he felt the level of anxiety which was pulsating through him like a recurring electric shock! Life had just got a whole lot more interesting and Barry's anxiety was right at the surface! There was no latency to it! He was afraid. Afraid of the unknown. Afraid of what David might do. Afraid of how the rest of the Board would respond if he raised the issue with them. He feared the worst; that he would in fact lose the battle with David and be forced to resign. Then what? So many questions, so few answers.

He had less than a week to prepare for the upcoming Board meeting and as was the usual expectation, written into his job description in fact, he was to lead the devotional, setting the tone for the Board meeting. Being a person of strong convictions and personal integrity, Barry knew he couldn't just deliver the perfunctory devotional. He would have to lay it all on the line, exposing what had transpired in the privacy of his office. Consulting his two closest friends, both accountability partners, he received the assurance and encouragement from them that he needed to raise the issue in the course of his devotional at the Board meeting. In spite of their support and encouragement, he knew that he was putting his job on the line. If this went poorly, it would all be over. In spite of the anxiety he felt and the legitimate fears which fuelled his anxiety, Barry knew this was a hill worth dying on. How could God honour the manipulative tactics employed by David and bless the ongoing ministry of the church? Barry knew he wasn't a perfect pastor but there were ways of addressing genuine concerns and issues, and David's approach didn't fit the pattern and teaching of Scripture. Barry thought he would have the support of the rest of the Board, but he wasn't 100% sure. He couldn't poll them in advance of the meeting. He would have to throw caution to the wind, and throw it he did, in spite of the anxiety and fear that kept him awake for parts of every night leading up to the Board meeting.

   He walked into the meeting more than a little apprehensive, but confident that what he was about to do was the right thing! He was prepared to face whatever the consequences might be coming out of the Board's response. As Barry prepared his devotional, he had written his thoughts down verbatim and he was committed to sticking to his notes. He did not want something taken out of context, twisted, and then used against him, something he was confident David would do if he felt it would advance his cause. In that event he would have his notes to fall back on.

The Anxious Congregation

When David asked Barry to lead in the devotional, he opened his Bible revealing his printed notes. Little did David realize what was about to be unfold. Reading from the Gospels, specifically the passage where Jesus referred to those things done in secret being brought into the light, Barry addressed the Board saying, "There are some things that have been taking place in secret that need to be brought out into the light." He proceeded to inform the rest of the Board regarding David's actions, including his meeting with the District Superintendent requesting that he find Barry another church, and the meeting less than a week prior where David had suggested Barry resign. "This is something you need to be aware and if there's an issue with my leadership I am more than prepared to talk about that with you as a group and deal with any issues that arise out of that discussion." With that Barry closed his Bible and waited, his heart racing a hundred miles a minute! He knew the meaning of anxiety in a whole new way.

The deafening silence only served to heighten his fears. Had he made a big mistake? Would he live to regret this decision? Would he be looking for a new place to do ministry? If so, how would he provide for his family? He knew that he had just laid down the gauntlet. He would either emerge from this meeting looking for another job, or he would have put the real issues on the table for all to see and begin to address, in the process perhaps having strengthened his leadership role in the church. Which way the scales would tip, Barry wasn't sure. He was sure he had done the right thing. He knew that doing the right thing didn't always feel good, and what felt good wasn't always the right thing to do. He knew that doing the right thing sometimes meant facing your fears and anxiety and moving ahead anyway. What he wasn't prepared for was what transpired next!

After what seemed like an eternity of silence, but was actually less than a minute, one by one, each of the board members challenged David, calling into question his actions and challenging his authority to engage such conversation and the course of action he had attempted to orchestrate. Barry was dumbfounded! He couldn't believe his ears! He was certain this kind of frank and honest conversation had rarely (if ever) taken place at Grenwich, let alone with David Hill. One of the Board members known to be an independent thinker and a good, strong leader, looked straight at David and said, "If there's a leadership issue in this church, it involves all of us as a Board, not just Barry." With that Barry knew that he was going to be okay. Suddenly a host of fears began to subside and his anxiety started to abate. But the conversation continued and David's face turned redder with each additional rebuke.

The last person to speak was the lone woman on the male dominated Board. In a soft but very firm voice she looked straight at David and said, "You don't represent me in your actions, and I no longer trust you!" You could have heard a pin drop! David reached for an envelope inside his Board binder, threw it on the table and said, "Here's my resignation! I was going to submit it at the end of the meeting, but you can have it now!" With that he stormed out of the Board meeting. The silence was deafening, lasting for what seemed like another eternity. Barry and the Board sat in stunned disbelief, reflecting on what had just transpired. Barry did not find the silence helpful in keeping his fears in check or in stemming his anxiety. The longer the silence persisted, the more his fears began to surface and the more his anxiety increased.

Finally, after about 10 minutes the longest serving Board member, who wasn't a "yes" man by any stretch of the imagination, broke the silence. "Barry is at least the third, if not the fourth pastor David has done this to!"

The other Board members, all newer to the congregation, couldn't believe what they had just heard. "You're not serious?" queried one of them. "I know it for a fact!" was the reply. This did nothing to dispel their disbelief. Turning to Barry, one of them posed the same question Barry had posed to David less than a week previous: "Is this something the District Superintendent could help us with?" Barry was encouraged by the question. At least the first response wasn't a call for his resignation. "I asked David the same question, but he stonewalled me, saying that he didn't think the District Superintendent could really offer much in the way of help. I also reminded him that we had a process outlined in our constitution which provided a framework to deal with issues in my leadership and that we should talk about it as a Board. David told me that he was afraid that someone would call for a vote of confidence. I told him that I was prepared to live with that. If I didn't have the support of the people, I would respect that. But, if I did have their support, David should respect that. It didn't matter what I proposed, David refused to consider it."

There, he had done it! He had faced some more of his fears and said what he felt needed to be said. He had brought even more stuff into the light of day and he felt he had done it in a way that wasn't disrespectful of David but had laid it out as fact. In spite of his fear and anxiety, he had done what he felt was right! Why did it have to be so hard?

Within the next few minutes the Board made two key decisions which immediately reassured Barry and gave him some hope that they would begin dealing with the real issues that had been fuelling David's back-room antics. He knew they were about to set a new course of direction as to how

Grenwich would deal with these kinds of issues in the future. They agreed to contact Larry Harding, District Superintendent and ask him to facilitate a meeting to discuss these developments, and they very firmly instructed Barry that he was to have nothing to do with David, not even a conversation. "You let us deal with David on this. If you have any conversations with him, make sure someone else is there with you. This is our issue to deal with, not yours!"

Once again, Barry could not believe his ears! Not only did he still have a job, he had a group of leaders who were really going to bat for him and more importantly, for the church! Barry knew the implications of their decisions extended far beyond his own tenure as pastor. He knew this was a watershed mark that would determine the long term direction of the church. By virtue of their decisions, the leadership were clearly indicating they were prepared to pay the personal price to do what was right. They were willing to walk headlong into their collective anxiety, but little did they or Barry know what that price would be, and the length of time they'd have to live in the resultant anxiety!

Appreciative of the support he was experiencing, yet profoundly aware that this was not over yet, Barry offered, "I know that at some point I will need to sit down and talk with David. I'm willing to do that, but I am going to submit myself to you as leaders. When you think the time is right, you let me know and I'll be willing to meet. Until then, I will let you handle it."

Brian Ramsey was selected by the remaining Board members to act as interim Chair of the Board given David's resignation and hasty exit. They requested that Brian contact Larry Harding, the District Superintendent to arrange a meeting with the Board so that they could begin to strategize a proactive plan moving forward. They left the meeting not fully comprehending the magnitude of what had just transpired, nor how heated the battle would get in the days and weeks to come.

Barry headed for home, feeling spent emotionally, spiritually, and physically. On the other hand he felt a huge sense of relief and a relative peace. He was somewhat aware of how important this meeting had been, but completely unaware of what yet lay in front of him as a pastor, and what lay ahead of them as a church. As hard as it had been, he was relatively confident that he had done what was right, done what he felt God was calling him to do. At the end of the day, what mattered most to Barry was whether or not he was responding to Jesus' "follow me" call.

For Reflection and Discussion

1. What thoughts and feelings get stirred up as you read this chapter? What do you feel towards Barry? David? The rest of the Board?

2. What do you learn about the ongoing congregational system at Grenwich? How did others enable and facilitate a David Hill to continue operating in unhealthy ways? What clues are evident in the story? What strongholds were broken?

3. If this situation were to happen in your church, how do you think your leadership team would respond? If you were a member of the Board, how would you respond? What fears would get stirred up in you if you were Barry and had to bring this issue up in your congregation?

4. Why do you think pastors and church leaders have a difficult time standing up for what is right and doing what is right? What's at stake for you to do that?

5. In what ways is failing to do what's right a violation of the greatest commandment to love God and love other people? In what ways is it also a refusal to respond to Jesus' "follow me" call?

Chapter 7
The Main Thing – Loving God and Loving People

Try to put yourself into that meeting! Yes, it actually happened the way I've told it here - not one detail changed other than the names! Imagine what that might have been like for Barry, David, and the other Board members. What would you have done? What fears would you have been in touch with? How would you have managed your anxiety? Tried to stuff it? Ignored it? Sat quietly? Put it all on the table? I can almost guarantee you would have been acutely aware of your fear and anxiety given the historic patterns of Board interactions at Grenwich!

Rest assured the optimum time to wrestle with these sorts of questions is long before you find yourself in the situation. It's important to have done some of the hard reflective work of determining how you measure what matters, more importantly, determining what really matters, to Jesus and not just you, and to do that work long before you find yourself in a situation like what Barry found himself in. It's even better to have begun testing some of that in much less intense, real life situations.

But life doesn't always afford that luxury. Sad to say, the thought of living life that way stirs more anxiety than most committed Christ-followers are willing to live with, and raises more fears than they dreamed possible. And yet that's a key aspect of what Jesus' "follow me" call entails. Jesus' call to "follow me" will always surface anxiety and raise fears because it will stretch us. Our natural bent is to choose our own path, which is always an easier path, not the path of Jesus. To choose his path always costs us something, so wrestling with Jesus' call is important if we're serious about following him.

When asked to quantify what really matters, to identify the most important of all the Old Testament Commandments, Jesus adeptly wrapped two into one, love God and love people. What Jesus is saying is that whatever else we measure, we must keep the main thing the main thing, and if we're going to measure anything it ought to be the main thing, which is our practise of loving God and loving people and not our good intentions of loving God and loving people. If we want to know how we're doing we must measure our practise of loving God and loving people. But what does that look like in the context of a local congregation? An anxious local congregation? A fearful local congregation? A lot different that most of us think!

The Call to Love God and Other People

In Mark 12:28-34 we find Jesus engaged in an intense debate with the religious leaders. Their motivation wasn't to grow in their spiritual understanding. Their motivation was to back Jesus into a corner, force him to think on his feet in the hope that he would stick his foot in his mouth, with no graceful means of extracting it. We find a teacher of the law sitting back, observing the debate no doubt impressed with the collective wisdom of his colleagues. Mark tells us that he was even more impressed with Jesus' response as Jesus refused to bite the bait put before him. So this teacher of the law decides to take his best shot at Jesus. "Jesus, of all the 613 Old Testament commandments, which is the greatest?" In other words, "Which commandment is so basic and fundamental that all other commandments hang on that one?"

This question was not unusual because the religious leaders were constantly trying to rank the commandments from greatest to least. The greater the personal cost or sacrifice required for violation of a commandment, the greater the importance given to it. To devout Jews, the measure of one's spirituality was the degree to which one could keep those commandments deemed more substantive and important. The underlying assumption was that individual acceptance before God was possible through human achievement.

It is reasonable to assume that this teacher of the law prided himself on his ability to articulate all 613 of the Old Testament religious laws. It's equally reasonable to assume he would point to his own human ability to flawlessly keep most of those laws, at the very least those he deemed most important. He probably had his own ranking of the commandments and no doubt was somewhat surprised by Jesus' response.

Respecting Jewish religious tradition, albeit adding his own little twist to it, Jesus goes back to the foundation of Jewish religious devotion as found in Deuteronomy 6:4-9: "Hear O Israel, the Lord our God, the Lord is One." Every Jewish person serious about his or her religious practice would begin and end each day with the recitation of this phrase. It was a reminder of God's uniqueness, that He was the true God. In fact in the Jewish tradition, the emphasis falls on the fact that there is only one God. But it also served as a reminder of God's gracious favour in extending covenant love to Israel, "Hear O Israel, the Lord OUR God." Jesus says, "If you want to summarize all of the commandments into one overarching principle it is this: there is only one God" and in doing so,

Jesus called this religious leader back to his own spiritual roots. Jesus very quickly follows with, "And you must love the LORD your God with all your heart, all your soul, all your mind, and all your strength.' The second is equally important: 'Love your neighbour as yourself.' No other commandment is greater than these."

Jesus was calling this man to a passionate pursuit of relationship, first of all with God, and secondly with his fellow human beings. Notice how Jesus phrases it; since God is one, since there is only one God, then love him with the sum total of who you are. Notice how many times the word "all" is repeated, and notice what the word "all" modifies.

Jesus calls this man to pursue relationship with God with the totality of his physical capacities, the totality of his intellectual capacities, the totality of his spiritual capacities, the totality of his emotional capacities. What you have here is a call to a passionate, almost impulsive relational pursuit of God. Jesus brings this religious teacher to a crisis point: On the one hand he knows his own religious tradition; on the other hand, he hears Jesus' call to him. He must decide which road he will choose to go down? Jesus calls this religious leader and demands a passionate, all-consuming, unconditional relational pursuit of God. Talk about a relational redesign! This call to love God passionately was a call to a kind of love which would radically dictate the disposition of this man's life.

Jesus' call to this man was not only a call to pursue that kind of relationship with God, but with other people as well. Jesus was saying that a whole-hearted passionate pursuit of relationship with God will always find expression in a selfless concern for the people one comes in contact with. In this second command, "Love your neighbour as yourself," Jesus has in view people as they are, sinners who love themselves more than they love other people. It's more than a casual self-centred love that Jesus has in mind. He sees people here who have a love that is passionately, often impulsively self-directed and self-centred. What Jesus is saying to this religious teacher is this: "You are impulsively committed to taking care of yourself first and not worrying about anyone else. You are passionate in your commitment to protect yourself in a selfish way rather than give yourself selflessly in relationship. Now take that same intense passionately motivated self-love and redirect it towards your fellow human beings!" Jesus turns this kind of love on its ear and redirects the focus.

A typical application of this text goes something like this: "I can only love other people this way once I feel good about myself, once I have received inner healing for my own poor self-image." That is not what Jesus is talking about at all! He is talking about the part of this religious teacher that manifested with each waking breath his passionate commitment to love himself.

In addressing the religious teacher, Jesus is addressing you and me because we are no different. Jesus is talking about the obsessive, passionate, self-indulgent love that is a part of every one of us; the love that manifests itself in a stubborn commitment to protect ourselves at all costs, the love that manifests itself in a commitment to take care of our own interests ahead of the interests of others. So, in response to the question, "Which is the most important commandment?" Jesus calls this man to a passionate, all-consuming pursuit of a love relationship with God and other people. In calling the religious leader to that kind of passionate pursuit of God, Jesus calls you and me to that same kind of passionate pursuit of a love relationship with God and other people. They are inseparably linked. To love God the way Jesus envisions it is to love other people. It's not an either/or, it's a both/and!

Ken Thiessen

Jesus – What Loving God Looks Like

I don't know about you, but I do know about me. I learn better when I can see a principle like this illustrated. So if we want to see someone who embodies the passionate pursuit of a love relationship with God and other people the way it's laid out in this text, who can you and I look to? Well, what if we look to Jesus?

Look at Jesus as a twelve year old boy in Jerusalem, together with Mary and Joseph for the celebration of the Passover. Notice twelve year old Jesus dialoguing with the religious leaders in the temple, astonishing them with the depth of his questions and his understanding of spiritual truths, so much so that he misses the rendezvous appointment. Look at Jesus' response to a typical parent's concern, "Mom and Dad! Don't you get it? Don't you know why I came to this earth? Don't you know that I'm on a mission, and this is part of it?"

Look at Jesus responding to temptation in the wilderness. "Jesus, you haven't eaten in a long time. Why don't you just take these rocks and turn them into bread. You've got the power." Rather than exercise his power to satisfy his own legitimate desires independent of God's call on his life he responds, "Man shall not live by bread alone!"

"Jesus I have an easier way. You don't have to pay that high a price. You know, Jesus, God must not really love you very much if he's going to make you pay that kind of a price. Jesus I have an easier way for you to get the power. All you have to do is bow down here and worship me. Nobody will even know It will be just between you and me, and then the power is yours!"

Jesus' reply? "Worship the Lord Your God and serve Him only."

"Jesus, why don't you just jump from this peak? If God loves you as much as he says he does, then he won't let you fall to the ground. Surely he'll dispatch one of his angels to sweep you up before you hit the ground. And just think of how the people will respond to you when they see this! Jesus, just think about it! You will have all of these people eating out of the palm of your hand. They will want to follow you because they will see your supernatural powers."

Jesus' reply? "Do not put the Lord your God to the test."

The essence of each temptation was to test Jesus' resolve to passionately pursue that love relationship with God.

Look at Jesus in the Garden of Gethsemane. "Dad, I can't handle this anymore! I know what's coming. I know how much it's going to hurt, how humiliating it's going to be, how much it's going to break my heart to know that I have given myself so totally to this mission and the people and religious leaders just don't get it. Dad, I don't want to go through with it. It hurts too much; the price is too great! Dad, can you hear me, do you hear what I'm saying? Do you feel my pain? Dad, I really don't want to go through this, but I'm going to trust you with this. If there's no other way, then I'll do it!"

Look at Jesus as he endures the torture and crucifixion. "Dad, this is getting so bad. They're so cruel! My head hurts from the beating they've given me, and this cross is so heavy to carry. Dad, it hurts so much as they drive these nails through my hands and my feet. I can feel each blow. Ouch, it hurts as they drop this cross into the hole. It hurts so much to be hanging here like this. It hurts so much to see them mocking me like they are. Look at how hard this is for my family, and for those who have given everything to follow me.

Dad, where are you? Do you care about me at all? This hurts too much. Dad why have you left me too? IT IS FINISHED."

That sure looks a lot like someone who was passionately committed to pursue relationship with God! When you want to know what that looks like lived out you need look no further than Jesus himself.

Jesus - What Loving Others Looks Like

Perhaps then Jesus is also the ultimate example of what loving other people looks like. What do we see in Scripture?

Let's start by looking at how he related to the disciples. I've already suggested they were a motley crew. You have Thomas who doubted and questioned everything, James and John who were more concerned about their own agenda than God's, Peter the loud-mouth know–it-all, and Judas the betrayer. Jesus never wrote them off and never bailed on the relationship, as tempting as I'm sure it must have been at some points. Not even Judas! Jesus served him by washing his feet just like he washed the rest of their feet. John tells us that the best way Jesus could show his love for them was in serving them!

Look at Jesus' interaction with the Samaritan woman at the well, someone who in that culture had at least three strikes against her; she was a woman, a Samaritan, she was divorced multiple times and the man she was currently with wasn't her husband. Jesus not only talked to her, something which broke all the cultural norms, he offered her a taste of the kingdom and the living water that he would soon make available to all.

Notice Jesus' interaction with Mary Magdalene, the prostitute who came and washed his feet. Everyone else was offended by not only her actions, but her very presence! Jesus didn't rebuke Mary Magdalene, but rebuked everyone else who looked down on her in judgment!

How about Matthew and Zacchaeus who were dishonest, disreputable tax collectors. Rather than judge them, he called one to be his disciple and invited himself to dinner with the other, a significant cultural expression of unconditional acceptance and friendship.

Observe Jesus' interactions with the religious people like the individual in text. In Jesus' interactions with religious types he always called them to live consistent with their professed beliefs, exposed their hypocrisy, challenged their religious legalism, and redirected their misguided passion. Ironically he reserved his harshest condemnation for the religious types who refused to wrestle honestly with his call to love God and love others. He showed his greatest compassion and acceptance to those who society labelled as undesirable or outcast.

Jesus accepted people where they were at but loved them too much to leave them there. He called them to something more. Often we judge people for where they're at and will only "love" them when they behave and/or believe right, which is totally opposite to Jesus.

In response to the religious teacher's question, Jesus connected two commandments in an inseparable way: "There is no commandment (singular) greater than THESE (plural)." The teacher's response to Jesus? "You're right. It's more important than offering empty sacrifices; it's more important than keeping the other 611 commandments." As much as the teacher knew it in his head, did he know it in his heart? Did he get it to the point where he was ready to live it out and allow it to radically alter the trajectory of his life?

As Jesus extended this call to the religious teacher he was calling him to something which Jesus himself was willing to embody. He was in essence saying, "Love God, love people, and do as you please." You may say, "Isn't that dangerous?" My response to you would be, "What are you afraid of?" Whether you're conscious of it or not, a question like that exposes your fear and anxiety. If my greatest motivation in life is to passionately love God and love other people with the sum total of my being, and to love in that order, that's going to frame the "do as I please" part, and I'll probably be okay.

If Jesus were to look at our hearts, strip away our involvement in our own religious rituals, what would he say to you? To me? The heart of the matter, Jesus says, is the matter of your heart. Notice that he doesn't say that the heart of the matter is the matter of our religious rituals or even the passionate pursuit of them. He doesn't say that the heart of the matter is how we do adhering to the other 611 commandments or how we enforce those on others. Would he say to people like you and me what he said to the religious teacher, "You are not far from the kingdom" or would he say, "You are far from the kingdom"?

When you begin to reflect Jesus' call as it relates to anxious congregations, you carve an interesting route through most local churches! Anxious congregations don't appear on the surface to be unloving. Most would vehemently justify their actions as a more complete expression of the kind of love Jesus called people to live out. They would profess their love for God and other people and suggest their anxious reactivity is motivated by that love. David Hill would certainly have professed his love for God and other people as would those who passively sat back and enabled a David Hill to continue to wield power over the people of Grenwich Community Church.

But when you get beneath the surface, what you discover is that their actions are motivated by the self-centred, self-protective love Jesus exposed in the religious teacher. As much as David Hill suggested he was trying to "protect" Barry from a vote of confidence, the deeper motivation was about managing David's anxiety and retaining the control he had enjoyed for so many years at Grenwich! To open up the "can of worms" in a broader context would make it much more difficult to manage his anxiety and he couldn't control the outcome. The fear of that possibility motivated his actions, regardless of his verbal professions to the contrary. Anxious congregations at their core are far less loving, of God and other people, than what they profess. They are far less aware of how unloving they really are. They are most often motivated by self-protective, self-serving self-love and not the sacrificial kind of love that Jesus modelled and calls them to live into! That self-protection is motivated by fear. To choose something other than self-protection leaves them vulnerable and exposed. That's not to say they're not well-meaning in their efforts! So was the religious teacher who posed the question to Jesus. His sincerity was not the issue. The bigger issue was whether his sincerity was misdirected or misinformed.

I believe that you're not that much different than the religious teacher in that you are sincere, but probably misdirected and misinformed in your sincerity. I'm just like you so I'm not here to sit in judgment. I do want to invite you to reflect more deeply on the application of Jesus' call to the context of your own life and that of your congregation. If God is looking for people who are willing to passionately love Him and other people, is that a cause you think is worth dying for? Really? Jesus did! If it's not worth dying for, is it worth living for? Like you I desperately want to say a hearty, emphatic "yes!" to that but reflect with me a bit more.

As you think about your local congregation, I'm sure there are situations and people that you know should be addressed.

You're not the only one who knows it. Intuitively most people share your sense. Some of those situations have gone unaddressed for years, in some cases generations! I wonder why it is that so many good, sincere people quietly sit by (the silent majority) and allow these situations to continue to hamper body life under the guise of "loving God and other people"?

I know what it's like. It's tough to be the one to step into some of those situations. They are political and relational minefields. You're never quite sure when you're going to step on the next improvised explosive device! You're not quite sure what the response is going to be. You're not sure whether or not it will make a difference. It might hurt someone's feelings! I get that, but guess what. That's anxiety talking! Your anxiety! Your fears! In order for you to do the loving thing, you're going to have to face your anxiety and your fears, name it for what it is, and move into it! And pay the price to do so. There's always a price to pay. But back to Grenwich!

For Reflection and Discussion

1. What's your reaction to the characterization of what loving God and loving other people looks like as lived out by Jesus?

2. If Jesus' example were what your church followed in your collective efforts to love God and other people, how would life be different? For you? For your church?

3. If loving other people involves speaking the truth in love in difficult situations, what fears get stirred up? Individually? As a church?

4. List some examples (personal and as a church) of what you thought was a loving response but upon reflection was probably more self-protective than self-sacrificing?

5. What tangible steps can you take individually and as a church to love God and other people more fully?

Ken Thiessen

Chapter 8
Grenwich - What's Love Got to Do With It?

Early the next morning Larry Harding received a call from Brian Ramsey, the newly appointed interim chair of the Grenwich Board. Barry had briefed Larry prior to the meeting regarding his plan of action, so the call didn't come as a complete surprise. Larry was given an overview of the developments and outcome of the previous night's meeting. Brian asked if he would be able to meet with the Board to help them debrief the events that had transpired, and strategize a plan moving forward. They agreed to meet on the following Tuesday. Brian's next call was to Barry, informing him of the meeting. Barry was relieved that finally something was going to be done about all that had taken place "in secret" over the past three months.

While Barry felt a sense of relief and hope, on other fronts, the battle was intensifying. News of David's resignation spread like a wildfire through Grenwich and the community. David did his part to fan the flames, adding his own slant which made him appear to be the victim of a power-hungry pastor. There were some who hung on his every word, supportively rallying around him, determined to "protect" the church from certain demise. What was really at stake was David's grip on power, a grip that had its hands firmly wrapped around the figurative neck of the church, strangling it to death. Some knew it, but few had the courage to step in and confront David. Perhaps they knew the price they would have to pay. Barry was aware that his predecessor had tried to address David's grip on power, but when push came to shove, there wasn't a critical mass of other leaders who were willing to name, own, and walk into their own anxiety and join him in charting a different future.

Barry went about his weekly pastoral duties and began his sermon preparation for the upcoming Sunday service, but it was hard to stay focused. Lingering ever close to the surface were the events of that pivotal Board meeting. While at one level he felt a sense of relief, on another level he was filled with self doubt. Had he really done the right thing? Was that really the "loving" thing to do? Where would the dust finally settle in terms of life at Grenwich? What would the future look like? There were more questions than answers, and the questions only served to peak his anxiety, and intensify his fears.

As Barry arrived for church on Sunday, David was noticeably absent. Whispering in the foyer served to heighten the drama of the events which had unfolded during the week. To say that Barry had butterflies in his stomach would have been to grossly understate the obvious. This feeling, and many others more intense than this, would become the norm as Barry stood to preach each week.

He became keenly aware that with each word that dropped from his lips, invisible daggers were being directed his way from some sitting in front of him. David, not present in body, was very much present in spirit. If Barry didn't believe in "ghosts", he would quickly learn a lesson about their existence and the power of their influence. The "ghost" of David Hill was very much alive and well at Grenwich, and there was an accompanying spiritual power to it. This was another reality seminary could never have prepared him for. There was no shortcut to learning this lesson first-hand, other than in the trenches of real life!

Barry got through that first service but it took a huge emotional and spiritual toll on him. Only a handful of people really knew the toll it took on him, Diane, and their kids. While Barry and Diane did their best to shield the kids from the full impact of all that had transpired, the kids knew something was up. But for Barry, it was another hurdle he had crossed and he was on to the next. He knew that he could not wilt under the pressure. Well, he could wilt, but he was making the hard choice not to. This would be a direct test of his ability as a leader and a pastor, and the stakes were monumental; personally, professionally, and organizationally for the church. Barry was aware of this, and he knew he was on the front lines of spiritual warfare. He also knew he was not alone. He had people who were standing with him, walking with him as he engaged the front lines of battle.

The Grenwich Board reconvened the following Tuesday for their first formal gathering since the fateful meeting a week earlier. District Superintendent Larry Harding was present to provide support, perspective, and counsel to Barry and the leadership team. Larry briefed the Board on his meeting with David, where David had requested his help in facilitating Barry's "call" to another congregation. Board members were again surprised to hear in more detail the unilateral and brazen nature of David's actions. Brian provided Larry with more details regarding the previous week's Board meeting, which set the tone for an open, frank, and forward-thinking conversation and dialogue.

As difficult as that meeting was, there was an energy that pulsated through each person present. They were wrestling to discern more fully what it meant to love God and love other people, in the midst of the turmoil they were all living through. There was also a collective willingness to pay the personal, emotional, and spiritual price required to do what was right.

For the most part, Barry was an observer in the meeting. He knew this was not his battle to fight. In spite of that, he too was energized by the interaction! He realized that a new paradigm was being formed, one that would shape the way Board interaction, decision-making, congregational input, and accountability was lived out in the context of Grenwich. He felt supported by the leadership's commitment and was thankful they were willing to step up to the plate in strong and dynamic ways, motivated by their desire to love God and love all of the people of Grenwich, David Hill included!

Several important decisions and outcomes emerged from that meeting. Larry was unwavering in his reassurance and support of Barry and the Board. They had done the right thing in putting the underlying issues on the table, and in challenging David Hill. They had not allowed their individual or collective fear and anxiety to hold them hostage, but had in fact acted in love. They had done what was best for all concerned, for David Hill, the Board, Barry, and Grenwich. Even if it didn't look like love or feel like it, they had done the loving thing! More importantly they had done what was best for the cause of the Kingdom. Their actions were motivated by a desire to love God and love other people even if it was hard, cost them something, and even if they were afraid. Each of them had paid a price. Collectively they had paid a price. What they didn't realize was that their collective decision would forge a new bond of friendship among them as a group. They would learn more fully what it meant to really love God and love other people as the process continued to unfold.

Another somewhat startling development coming out of the meeting was Larry's acknowledgement that denominational leaders had been well aware of David's tactics. They knew this had been his longstanding behavioural pattern. In spite of that awareness, the voluntary, autonomous association of churches with the denomination often left denominational leaders in a quandary, not sure how best to respond. The only "authority" leaders like Larry had in working with local congregations was contingent on the established relational capital with either the pastor or the church Board. David Hill had been the gatekeeper to ensure that relational capital never extended beyond himself! That "rule" was now clearly broken and Larry was fully prepared to build relational capital in a way that would lay a new foundation for denominational input and resourcing to Grenwich! That was good news to the Board, and Barry!

The Board also agreed that Brian Ramsay and Randy Mann should attempt to meet with David Hill to further the conversation about his actions and debrief the events of the previous week's meeting. Larry Harding was asked to serve as a broker of sorts to arrange and participate in the meeting. The Board anticipated that David might be resistant to such a meeting given that they had individually and collectively challenged his actions and called him to account. Larry's help was important in the process. Barry again reaffirmed his willingness to meet with David, if and when the Board and Larry felt it appropriate or helpful.

In the community, word was continuing to spread as to what had transpired the previous week. Almost overnight "anonymous" became the predominant surname on the church membership roll! Concerns regarding Barry's leadership were surfacing with some regularity from "anonymous" members. No one could ever remember receiving "anonymous" into membership, but virtually overnight, the whole "anonymous" family (cousins, uncles, aunts, grandparents, wannabe family members) had joined the membership ranks of Grenwich! Barry was sure this was another manifestation of the ghost of David Hill!

It wasn't long before Barry received a visit from a retired pastor in the congregation, a mentor of sorts. When Barry arrived at the church to commence ministry, he had connected with this pastor, seeking to learn from his wisdom and years of ministry experience. As time went on, what became apparent was this relationship was stretching them both. Their respective ministry paradigms were built on some fundamentally different foundational principles, and the differences had begun to surface.

On this particular visit he too informed Barry that there were "anonymous" concerns about his leadership and he felt the "loving" thing to do was pass them along to Barry. Barry engaged him in theological dialogue suggesting that to cloak the concerns behind the unnamed "anonymous" church member was really to go against the teaching of Scripture. Barry contended that Jesus' teaching was clear. If you have an issue with a person go to that person directly so that the matter can be resolved. If those attempts are unsuccessful, then involve others in seeking resolution of the matter and reconciliation.

"Barry, people are afraid to come and talk to you," the retired pastor said.

Barry responded, "Encourage them to bring someone along with them. I'll meet with anyone who wants to meet with me so that we can talk about it and grow together. I'm not saying I'm a perfect pastor, and I assume some of the concerns are probably valid and legitimate. But unless I hear first-hand what the concerns are, how can I respond in a way that's appropriate and constructive? Unless I know the specific nature of the concerns, how can I ever really be sure as to whether or not I'm addressing the real or the right issues and concerns? If we as leaders can't live out Jesus' call to express concerns and deal with conflict face to face, how can we ever expect the congregation as a whole to live it out?"

What Barry wasn't prepared for was the response. "Barry, I know that's what Scripture says, but that's not how it works in reality!"

Barry was dumbfounded, shocked, amazed, and profoundly disappointed at what he had just heard! This had come from the lips of an ordained minister, a former denominational leader, someone who would have professed the authoritative nature of Scripture in matters of faith and practice. Yet here, in one fell swoop, his statement belied his verbal pronouncements to the contrary. Catching his breath and composing himself, Barry calmly but emphatically replied, "If that's what Scripture calls us to, then my job as a pastor is to make sure I live that out and call others to do the same."

With that, the meeting came to an abrupt conclusion. Barry intuitively knew, however, that the subject matter of that meeting would makes its way directly to David Hill before the day was done!

Barry wasn't the only one receiving reports of "anonymous" concerns related to his leadership. The Board was receiving similar reports. The systemic anxiety was spreading under the guise of "loving God and loving people" by "protecting" the identity of the sources. In reality, the fear of face to face dialogue regarding difficult issues was the bigger motivator behind the protective cloak of anonymity! As the Board met for their first full meeting following Larry Harding's visit, they made a critical, game-changing decision. They decided to delete "anonymous" from the membership roll! No longer would they entertain concerns from members with the surname "anonymous"! They did NOT say they would not entertain concerns; they said they would not entertain "anonymous" concerns. They committed themselves to collectively address every concern brought to them by an individual or group of individuals who were willing to meet face to face, in accordance with the teachings of Jesus. They also quickly informed the congregation of their decision.

Several somewhat surprising developments surfaced as a result. Where once the volume of concerns had been portrayed as a raging river, that raging river mysteriously reduced to a mere trickle as if struck by an overnight drought! The response of leadership was consistent. "We're happy to meet with people face to face to discuss the concerns, but we will not entertain 'anonymous' concerns."

The other development was an increased number of reports of people on the verge of "leaving" Grenwich. The stated reason was Barry Moffat's leadership, and the rumour mill was rife with speculation as to who would be next. The big question in the local coffee shops was, "What's going on at Grenwich?"

In response, the leadership committed themselves to meeting with every individual or family who had left, or was considering leaving the congregation. The purpose of these meetings was twofold, to attempt to discern their reasons for leaving, and pray a blessing on them as they left, encouraging them to find another place for worship and fellowship. When contacted, many refused to meet, but where there was an openness and a receptivity, those meetings were for the most part cordial, heartfelt, and genuine. The leadership repeated the same message at each meeting. "We're sorry to see you go, but we want you to know the door is always open should you choose to return." They meant what they said, even to David Hill! Surely living out the "love God, love people" call of Jesus required no less from them.

With regard to David, a meeting had been arranged with Randy, Brian, and Larry to discuss some of what had transpired. As much as they were encouraged by David's willingness to meet, their hopes were quickly dashed when the meeting actually took place. David was unrelenting in his assertion that Barry Moffat had to go. There was no negotiating; it was going to be David's way, or the proverbial highway. What became even more apparent was David's deepening sense of entitlement in decisions pertaining to Grenwich. In his mind, his vote trumped all others. He considered himself "first among equals". It would have been more accurate to say he considered himself "first above equals"! He felt he deserved that because Grenwich owed its life to him. Hadn't he paid the bills when Grenwich had no money? That ought to be worth something! He never verbally expressed it that way, but the attitude of entitlement raged within him, and it was definitely reflected in his actions!

Larry Harding continued to engage David in personal dialogue, hoping desperately to see some progress in the discussions. Since there was at least one degree of separation between Larry and Grenwich, there wasn't the same level of acrimony in his conversations with David as what Brian and Randy had experienced. Larry continued to challenge David on his tactics, assumptions, and desired outcomes. He also persisted in his attempts to set up a meeting between himself, David, Barry, and members of the Board.

Over the course of several weeks Larry seemed to be making progress in his efforts to arrange a meeting. Finally, David agreed to meet and a date was set. Larry immediately contacted Barry to inform him of the date and confirm his availability to participate. As promised, Barry agreed immediately. As much as he had indicated his willingness to meet with David and submit to the leadership in terms of the timing of that meeting, that didn't serve to calm his anxiety. He knew it was right, but he could also feel his blood pressure rising the closer he got to the scheduled meeting. He was afraid of sitting face to face with the man who single-handedly had tried to oust him from his position as Lead Pastor of the church. He was afraid of the kind of venom that might spew from David should they be sitting across the table from each other. He was afraid that what David had said about him behind his back, he might now say to his face. Even if most of it proved to be untrue, it still wasn't something Barry looked forward to.

The morning of the scheduled meeting Barry received an interesting call from Larry Harding. "Barry, I got a call from David Hill last night and he has changed his mind about meeting together. He doesn't see the point of it and so the meeting is off!" Somehow Barry was not surprised. From his experience with David he knew there was little negotiating with David. If there ever appeared to be a softening in David's position, it was usually only a brief retreat so he could re-strategize and employ a different plan of attack. "Barry, you've done everything you can to try to resolve this. There's nothing more you can or need to do at this point in time. Let your Board handle it. You've got some real quality leaders there!" While Barry knew it was "over" he knew it wasn't really "over". Just because the meeting didn't happen, didn't mean that David wouldn't still do his best to accomplish his ultimate purpose! It would happen from the bushes rather than out in the open!

In the weeks since that pivotal Board meeting where all the cards had been laid on the table, David Hill had attended worship only once and that was the Sunday Barry Moffat was gone. David would never return to Grenwich, which in itself was not completely out of the ordinary. His father and his brother had left Grenwich under similar circumstances and David's father had been a charter member! They had left for similar reasons; their power base had been eroded and threatened. Sadly, when David's father passed away, the funeral was held in another local church. The family pride ran so deep that even in death they could not bring themselves to return to Grenwich.

Ironically, David and his wife began attending another church in the community where the pastor was the chair of the Board and WAS the Board. Somehow it had a hollow ring to it given his vociferous contention that Barry Moffat held too much power at Grenwich! Perhaps there was in fact a whole lot more at play in this situation than just Barry. Perhaps it was more about David than Barry. Perhaps it was more about David AND Barry, AND everyone else in the church!

For Reflection and Discussion

1. What external resources can your congregation access to help you deal with complex and difficult situations? Has your congregation ever brought in external resources to help you deal with a complex or difficult situation? Why or why not? What was the outcome?

2. Why do you think "anonymous" exerts so much influence on the life of a local congregation? What are some of the underlying factors which enable the unhealthy pattern to persist?

3. How does your congregation deal with "anonymous" concerns? What changes might you consider making to better manage the fear and anxiety present within your congregation?

4. What's your reaction to Larry Harding's acknowledgement that denominational leaders were aware of David Hill's history of "influencing" decision making at Grenwich? In what ways did denominational polity enable David's ongoing unhealthy influence in the church?

5. In what ways do you think responsibility for the historic patterns at Grenwich might extend beyond David to include Barry, and the rest of the congregation? Why do you think the easier "solution" is to focus exclusively on David?

Ken Thiessen

Chapter 9
The Language of Love Includes "Yes" AND "No"

I think you're beginning to see that loving God and loving people gets very complicated, as illustrated in life at Grenwich. I'm pretty sure that it's not a whole lot different in your church either. Wherever you are engaged in relationship with other people, the call to love God and love others is a complicated call to live out. Anxious congregations have some very interesting ways of defining what that looks like lived out!

I'm writing this while on a working vacation with my wife enjoying the sun, sand, and the ocean on Banderas Bay. It's a great reprieve from the onset of winter in the Canadian prairies where we make our home year round. Soaking in the sun by the pool, I've had opportunity to observe interactions between parents and children. There's an interesting pattern I've noticed. Hold on, this is an earth shattering, ground-breaking discovery! Kids experience and expect "yes" as the loving parental response and they experience "no" as something quite a bit less than a loving parental response. I bet you've never discerned that before! Of course you know I'm joking. Everyone who has ever observed parent/child interactions knows this to be true!

But here's a twist. Why is it that as adults we function in strikingly similar ways in our interactions with others, particularly in the church? Why do we feel that saying "no" in some inherent way violates God's call to "love" other people? Why do we assume that our unquestioned, non-reflective, almost impulsive "yes" is proof that we are living out God's call to "love" other people? Why do we experience God's "no" as an unloving response? Why do we rage at him for his "no!" as if we are somehow being treated harshly? Why do we so firmly believe that God must say "yes" to our every whim if he is indeed deemed to be "loving"?

If one of the primary hallmarks of love is to act toward another person motivated solely by that which is in their best interest, then depending on the context, "no" might in fact be the most loving response! Could it be that our misguided and "childish" notions about what loving God and loving people looks like lived out have more to do with the mismanagement of the anxiety and fear we experience in our relationships than they have to do with good, solid theological reflection? Have you ever considered the possibility that saying "yes" to other people sometimes makes it impossible to at the same time say "yes" to God? In fact, sometimes saying "yes" to people means we must say "no" to God! Other times saying "yes" to someone else might in fact be the least loving thing to do! Perhaps the language of love includes "yes" AND "no".

Jesus Knew How to Say "No"

Consider the example of Jesus who most fully encompassed what it means to love God and other people, and did it in a way that never compromised or sacrificed one for the other. Surprisingly, Jesus sometimes manifested his deepest love for God by saying "no" to people!

In Mark's Gospel the first glimpse we get of this is found in Chapter 1:35-39. "Before daybreak the next morning, Jesus got up and went out to an isolated place to pray. Later Simon and the others went out to find him. When they found him, they said, 'Everyone is looking for you.' But Jesus replied, 'We must go on to other towns as well, and I will preach to them, too. That is why I came.' So he traveled throughout the region of Galilee, preaching in the synagogues and casting out demons."

Don't let the familiarity or the brevity of the story distract you from the significance of what's going on here! Jesus' popularity and public appeal had skyrocketed. Were he to run for public office he would have topped the public opinion polls! He would have been the candidate of choice and it would have been a landslide! Not even close! Beyond that, he had begun to assemble his team by calling Peter, Andrew, James, and John. He had given people a taste of the "new" Kingdom that would be the focus of his message. He had done that by healing many of their diseases and freeing others from demonic control. His message and the power he possessed were unprecedented, so no wonder he was popular! Who wouldn't want to be associated with him? I would have probably been at the front of the line!

As Mark records it, Jesus had taken some alone time to connect with God and gain perspective in the midst of the heavy demands of ministry which is quite reasonable, if you ask me. The disciples, keenly aware of public sentiment and Jesus' popularity, came looking for him. Try to immerse yourself in the story and enter into the dynamics that ooze from the pages of Scripture. You can tell that the disciples were aghast at Jesus' apparent careless, insensitive, perhaps even selfish actions. "Everyone is looking for you!" Can't you just hear their incredulous tone laced with sarcasm and disbelief? "Jesus, don't you get it? People want to see you! They're lining up! What are you thinking?" Can you feel the intense demand and neediness behind their request? You get the sense that the only appropriate response from Jesus would be something along the lines of, "I'm sorry guys, I should have known better. Let's get going! We've got places to go and people to see!"

Bring this a little closer to home. You're on staff or in a leadership capacity at your church and a delegation comes imploring you to respond to some need they deem "urgent" in the life of your congregation. There's an implicit demand that you drop whatever else you are doing to attend to their demands! If you have been in any kind of leadership position in any organization, be it church, business, or nonprofit, you know this reality. You have lived it at least once and probably many more times! How do I know that? Every organization has a David Hill who feels his agenda supersedes everyone else's and they are more than free to let you know!

Do you feel the pressure to say "yes" to their demand? Do you feel the fear building as you contemplate their verbal and non-verbal response should you choose to do the unthinkable and say "no"? Do you catch their ridicule of you as a leader because you haven't already responded to the demand on your own? Maybe you haven't even noticed it! That only serves to intensify your feelings of inadequacy and self-doubt.

So what is the loving thing to do? How do you love God and love people in this situation without compromising one or the other? You wonder whether or not it's even possible. How do you determine what is truly best for them, for the church, for you? More importantly, how do you discern whether this is a ministry distraction, or a new ministry opportunity from God? These are all valid and important questions.

While you may never have thought about it this way, the flood of emotions pulsating through you as you contemplate your response is "anxiety speak". Probably a good part of what is motivating the urgency of the delegation's demand on you is their anxiety and they are committed to sharing it with you! Maybe someone passed it along to them and now they are re-gifting it to you! Remember, anxiety is the gift that keeps on giving, and giving, and giving. Not only are they committed to sharing it with you, now it is your job to do something about it, and to make it go away! The minute you do that, the transaction's complete. They have passed the "hot potato" of anxiety to you and it is all yours! Congratulations, you're the winner! Except you don't feel like a winner! They haven't really let it go either, because they're still monitoring your every move to ensure you are on the way to meeting their demands and doing so in a manner they approve of. So now the organization has at least one more anxious person than it did before, and that person is YOU!

Those are probably some of the dynamics at play in the exchange between Jesus and the disciples! I can hear someone say, "Jesus was never anxious!" I would contend that to be human is to know the experience of anxiety! Scripture is clear to remind us that while Jesus was fully divine, He was also fully human. The writer to the Hebrews reminds us that in Jesus we have a priest who can identify with us in our life experience, yet without sin. (Hebrews 4:15) Perhaps Jesus managed his anxiety in ways that were a whole lot healthier than what we are used to, and that made it seem like he was never anxious. But I contend he felt anxiety just like you and me. If not, we have a problem with what the writer to the Hebrews has to say. Anxiety is not the issue per se. It's what we do with the anxiety that is more important and in Jesus we see a healthy model of responding to and dealing with anxiety, both his, and others!

What's at stake for Jesus as he contemplates the disciples' request (really a demand) and his response? He can feel the anxiety pulsating from the disciples! They're frantic, "Jesus, we have to do something." More accurately, "Jesus, YOU have to do something!" Depending on how he responds he runs the risk of disappointing and/or frustrating the disciples and the crowds. Perhaps they will get angry with him! The disciples might decide that they are done with him. This wasn't going to be quite what they had envisioned it to be. What about the mission he's on? What about the call of his Heavenly Father who has sent him on this mission?

This passage oozes anxiety and yet in the midst of it Jesus appears profoundly calm, not unlike when he was sound asleep in the boat while the disciples cringed in terror, fearing for their lives as the storm raged around them! What a picture in contrasts! Jesus somehow able to manage his anxiety, while anxiety and fear was managing the disciples!

What is most interesting is Jesus' response. It's so casual, matter-of-fact, and almost nonchalant. At first glance it appears insensitive and unloving, at least the way most of us would define "love." Some of us might even call it rude!

His response is short and to the point, "No." It's not a reflexive, reactive "No". It is motivated by something far deeper, and more substantive. It is motivated by a clear understanding of his overall mission, and an understanding of something else he had already said "Yes" to. He knows that to say "Yes" to the demands of the disciples and the crowds is to begin the slippery slope of abandoning his "Yes" to God's call on his life. "We must go on to other towns as well, and I will preach to them, too. That is why I came."

There's no recorded response from the disciples but somehow I think there had to be one. I suspect none of them had the courage to verbalize it. But I am intrigued with their response none the less. I can imagine that bewilderment and shock would probably be accurate descriptors. I have to admit, they fit for me too! What was it about Jesus that enabled him to respond in such a calm, intentional, and determined manner when faced with the urgency emanating from the disciples?

Before we attempt to answer that question, let's look further at how Jesus encountered and interacted with other anxious people and situations. Let's pay attention to whom and what he said "Yes" to, as well as whom and what he said "No" to.

Earlier we looked at adolescent Jesus in the temple. Joseph and Mary have begun their trek back home only to discover their young son is nowhere to be found! Frantic with worry, they retrace their steps back to the temple where they find him calmly interacting with the religious leaders, oblivious to their parental angst! What normal parent wouldn't feel just as anxious given the same situation? Jesus' response? "Didn't you know I had to say 'Yes' to my Father?" In other words, mom and dad, that means "No" to you, but not in a precocious, defiant, or rebellious kind of way.

Notice Jesus in the wilderness offering a resounding "No" to each of the temptations posed to him. Not once, but three times! His motivation? A profound and deep desire to say "Yes" to God! Observe Jesus at the wedding in Cana. Mary, a typical mother, is concerned about the details and quickly notices that the host has run out of wine; which is a cultural and hospitality faux pax! Aware that Jesus possesses divine powers, she approaches him with a motherly piece of "information." "Jesus, did you know there's no more wine?" which translated means, "You have the power to do something, so DO it!" Jesus' response? "Dear woman, that's not our problem ... My time has not yet come." (John 2:4) Paraphrased only slightly that means, "No". There is no hint that Jesus' response is inappropriate, rude, or unloving. Mary, perhaps knowing something, instructs the servants to do whatever Jesus tells them. I'm not quite sure what that's about but she does it. Maybe it's a mother's intuition. Before long Jesus would offer a "Yes" in performing his first public miracle, turning water into wine.

How often did Jesus find himself in the temple in the presence of the religious establishment? His very presence caused their anxiety to bubble up! When he opened his mouth, their anxiety became a full-fledged tidal wave of emotion, often outrage! Unwilling to be controlled by their anxiety, he repeatedly defied and/or sought to redefine their religious traditions! Whether it was Sabbath observance, practice, and traditions, dietary laws, purification rituals, or social norms and customs, Jesus was repeatedly saying "No" which did little to earn him favour with the religious establishment. In essence Jesus offered a resounding "No", willing to face the anxious response and reaction, so that he could offer up a corresponding "Yes" to living out his calling to incarnate and usher in the Kingdom, inviting others to say "Yes" to it as well. His "No" was in fact the most loving thing he could have offered the religious leaders. If they had taken the time to serious reflect on what Jesus was saying and doing, they would have realized he was acting in their best interests, even if it didn't appear that way on the surface.

Several of the Gospels record encounters where people demanded a sign from Jesus, wanting proof that he was in fact the Messiah. Where and when a sign was demanded as a precursor to faith on the part of the recipient, Jesus never yielded to the demand. His answer was an emphatic "No" usually followed by a stinging rebuke of their hardness of heart.

Lest we think his "No" was reserved exclusively for those who were hard of heart, resistant to God or his message, Jesus also said "No" to people he cared deeply about, people he believed in. He said "No" to people who were sincere, respectful, committed followers. "Then the mother of James and John, the sons of Zebedee, came to Jesus with her sons. She knelt respectfully to ask a favour." Her request was simple. "In your Kingdom, please let my two sons sit in places of honour next to you, one on your right and the other on your left." (Matthew 20:20-21) She was at least respectful in her selfishness! She even said "Please!" Jesus' response was "No". He even tried to help James and John understand the full consequence of their mother's request. They glibly expressed their ability and willingness to face the consequence. In spite of their assurances, Jesus' response was still "No".

Perhaps one of the more poignant examples of Jesus' "No" is recorded by John. "A man named Lazarus was sick. He lived in Bethany with his sisters, Mary and Martha. This is the Mary who later poured the expensive perfume on the Lord's feet and wiped them with her hair. Her brother, Lazarus, was sick. So the two sisters sent a message to Jesus telling him, 'Lord, your dear friend is very sick.' But when Jesus heard about it he said, 'Lazarus's sickness will not end in death. No, it happened for the glory of God so that the Son of God will receive glory from this.' So although Jesus loved Martha, Mary, and Lazarus, he stayed where he was for the next two days." (John 11:1-6)

As much as Jesus knew what the final outcome would be, Mary and Martha didn't, so who is to blame them for their utter and complete confusion at Jesus' initial "No"? I'm certainly not going to be the one to cast aspersions on them because I would be right there with them questioning the wisdom of Jesus' "No", and questioning the basis and depth of the friendship. But Jesus said "No" and that meant Mary and Martha (and Lazarus) had to experience the grief and sting of death. By the time Jesus arrived two days later, Lazarus was dead. How could that have been a loving response? Did Mary and Martha experience Jesus' delay ("No") as an act of love? Even if it didn't feel like love to them, is it possible that it was in fact an act of love?

John continues the story. "When Martha got word that Jesus was coming, she went to meet him. But Mary stayed in the house. Martha said to Jesus, 'Lord, if only you had been here, my brother would not have died. But even now I know that God will give you whatever you ask.'" (John 11:20-22) Martha's very legitimate sadness and disappointment is obvious. If only...!

As I reflect on this, I am left with some questions. Why did Mary stay in the house and not come out to meet Jesus? Was she upset? Bitter? Trying to make a point? What did Martha "know" about Jesus' power? Did she really believe that Jesus could do something to bring Lazarus back to life now, before the final resurrection?

I am sure that after Jesus miraculously raised Lazarus from the dead many of their questions were answered and they knew love in a whole new experiential way! But in the process, Jesus had said "No" without in any apparent way compromising his love for God or other people!

Jesus Also Knew How to Say "Yes"

Jesus also knew how to say "Yes" and often did so in contexts that broke cultural norms, stereotypes, and expectations. Begin with the people he chose to be on his "team". Saying "Yes" to Matthew was no small thing. Despised by devout Jews because of his occupation as a tax collector, Jesus' choice of him, an emphatic "Yes" of sorts, must have turned more than a few heads! Why would Jesus choose a guy like that? A review of the Gospels reveals Jesus regularly having dinner with Matthew types; those who society (and the religious establishment) would view with suspicion, even disdain. It's not hard to see how his "Yes" would have been experienced by them as a loving response.

Jesus said "Yes" to people who fell outside the traditional parameters of Judaism. Whether it was the Roman officer (Matthew 8:5-13), a Gentile woman (Matthew 15:21-28), a leper (Mark 1:40-45), Jairus and the woman with the bleeding disorder (Mark 5:21-43), the Samaritan woman at the well who had been married multiple times, and was not married to the man she was currently living with, (John 4:1-38), Jesus' "Yes" broke all of the rules and gave new meaning to the extent and scope of divine love.

There were some other ways in which Jesus' "Yes" was revolutionary in its expression of love! His interaction with the religious leaders and the woman caught in adultery (John 8:1-11) involved both a "Yes" and a "No". In refusing to be caught in the trap set for him by the religious leaders, by throwing stones at this woman he was saying "No" to the traditional interpretation of Jewish law. At the same time he was saying a profound "Yes" to grace, something which must have come as a complete shock to not only the religious leaders, but the woman herself! In saying "Yes" to grace, he did however, extend a call to her to "go and sin no more!"

There is one more account of Jesus' "Yes" that merits mention and it has particular relevance to many a local church context. The further Jesus went in his earthly ministry, the more specific he was about the requirements of those who would be his followers. John records, "At this point many of his disciples turned away and deserted him." (John 6:66)

Jesus' response? "Yes, you can leave!" There were no attempts to coddle them; no attempts to dissuade them from leaving; no effort to soften the message or the approach in order keep a few more on board; no cow-towing to their demands. He respected their adult decision and allowed them to leave. No mention that perhaps his actions were in any way "unloving" or unkind either! Perhaps the most loving thing Jesus could do was respect their freedom of choice and do that without shaming them in the process. Jesus responded similarly to the rich young man who, when faced with the cost of following, walked away. Mark indicates that the rich man's question evoked a response of genuine love from Jesus. It is safe to assume Jesus' perspective did not change as he walked away. Perhaps Jesus' willingness to let him walk away was itself a profound expression of love.

Some Implications

What lessons can we learn from the example and practise of Jesus? What are the implications for how we interact in the context of a local church?

One of the first things we see is that "No" can be the most loving response in many situations. It's possible to say "No" in a way that remains relationally engaged with people. When Jesus said "No" he was able to maintain relational interaction with them, even when he disagreed most vehemently with their lifestyle choice, theological perspective, spiritual practise, or commitment level.

Too often our "No" is accompanied by relational distance and in some cases, relational alienation! Don't hear me say that is never an appropriate response. But too often, it is an anxious response because we are not really sure how to say "No" to people and deal with their reactive response. It is hard to stay fully engaged relationally with someone you care about who is angry with you for saying "No". If that person has developed a pattern of getting their way by using anger, you are simply the latest person in their sights. What makes it even more difficult is when others in your friendship circle are saying "Yes" more often than they should. Remaining relationally engaged in that kind of a situation occurs most effectively when you are able to manage the anxiety and fear before it manages you! Jesus knew how to do that and He shows us it is possible.

Jesus also said "No" to people he deeply cared about, people who mattered to him. We never get the sense that his response was motivated by a desire to manage his own anxiety, serve his own self-interest, or exact undue pain on the person on the receiving end. In fact, Jesus' "No" often increased the likelihood for his anxiety to spike, depending on the response of the individual or group. In doing so he provided something of a model for us to consider and follow.

Jesus was very clear as to the values which shaped his approach to life, his interactions with God, and with others. Those values had been shaped long before he found himself in a situation where someone else's anxiety was desperately seeking to consume him and dictate his response! Jesus was very clear in his ability to self-define and differentiate himself from the anxious demands of others. He did so in a way which was not motivated by a desire to shame or minimize the other person. Well, maybe there is at least one exception that is worth noting. I'm not sure he didn't attempt to shame the religious leaders; at least once! But he reserved that for those who were most hard-hearted, who had been given numerous opportunities to respond differently, but had chosen not to.

Given what we see lived out by Jesus, perhaps we need to re-examine, redefine, or expand our definition of "love" as it has been traditionally defined and lived out in the context of Christian community. Perhaps it is time to move beyond our childish ways in thinking that "No" is an unloving response and "Yes" is always a loving response. Perhaps it is time to acknowledge that anxiety and fear run at the core of our practise of love, influencing our actions and expressions of "love" much more than we care to admit or realize.

Let's go back to the scenario I posed at the beginning of this chapter, where a delegation has come to you with a demand that you act and do so in a way that meets their approval. You know that if you don't yield to their demands they will be upset. Their anxiety will continue to rage and yours will spike! It would definitely be easier to say "Yes" but it might in fact be more loving to say "No". It could be that their request is not in the best interest of the whole body. It might be inconsistent with the vision and mission the church has felt called by God to live into. It could be that their motivations are unduly selfish and self-serving. If you say "No" they might threaten to withhold their financial support, resign their volunteer involvements, and worse yet, leave the church! You know that I am not making this up because you've experienced it at least once, if not more. There are probably names and faces that immediately come to mind!

I have been in more than one church setting where the response from others has been, "Oh we can't let them leave! We have to do everything we can to make them change their minds! They've been long-term members here! What would we do without them? They give more than anybody else to support our church! How will we survive?" I know of one pastor who was told it was his pastoral duty and calling to make sure he did everything to keep people from leaving the church. When he challenged that notion, the sincerity and depth of his pastoral heart was called into question. The implicit message was, "If you were truly a loving pastor you would do what I am asking you to do and you would do it without hesitation!"

But I wonder; what do you think Jesus would do? I think Jesus would probably call it for what it is; childish. Perhaps more of what we pass off as "loving" behaviour in the church is little more than childish attempts to keep our anxiety in check, and avoid facing the fear of how people will respond to us if we really are "loving". In the process we say "Yes" to people and "No" to God. That is rarely our conscious motivation. I am suggesting that more often than not it is our deeper, non-reflective, reactive motivation. It is our attempt to manage our anxiety and fear (albeit in childish ways) under the guise of love; loving ourselves instead of the people we are professing to love.

What would Jesus do? I think he would say that not every "No" is unloving nor is every "Yes" loving. It depends on the context. We usually experience less anxiety if we frame life in black and white terms. Again, don't hear me saying that some things aren't black and white, but usually we extend the parameters for black and white significantly beyond what Scripture does, not unlike the religious leaders whom Jesus challenged so strongly! Legalism is often more about our childish attempts to manage anxiety and fear than it is about orthodoxy and orthopraxy. Living life in the reality of the full colour spectrum has its challenges and yet Jesus seemed quite content with "colour", more so than those who held rigorously to black and white legalism. The language of love really does include "Yes" AND "No". Context and motivation determines when either of these are truly loving responses!

For Reflection and Discussion

1. When have you seen someone say "Yes" under the guise of being "loving" when in fact their response might not have

been as "loving" as it appeared? When have you seen someone say "No" and it be a true expression of love?

2. When have you said "Yes" to someone when you really wanted to say "No" but didn't because you were afraid of their reaction? What was at stake for you to say "No"?

3. How would you say your congregation is doing in really loving people by saying both "Yes" and "No" and doing so in appropriate ways? Why do you think that is? If change is required, what factors might make change more difficult?

4. If the pastor and/or leadership in your congregation began saying "No" to the some of the many requests that come their way, what do you think would be the response? Would they have the support from others to withstand any potential backlash? Why or why not?

Ken Thiessen

Chapter 10
Grenwich - Framing a New Paradigm

While time had passed since the pivotal Board meeting and the immediacy of the David Hill scenario had begun to subside, things were far from normal at Grenwich. The systemic anxiety continued to bubble to the surface with great regularity, and many weren't even sure what "normal" looked like. While the historical definition of "normal" was certainly crumbling, the new definition had not yet been fully formed. The crumbling was causing anxiety and fear for long-term members. The Grenwich they had grown to love and appreciate was disappearing. The unknown of the present and the uncertain future were causing heightened anxiety for others. It was becoming increasingly more difficult to pretend that Grenwich wasn't an anxious congregation!

Barry too, found himself feeling new and different kinds of anxiety as he sought to provide leadership and input into framing the new "normal" that was emerging. While he was no longer afraid of what David Hill might be trying to orchestrate, he had a nagging fear that someone else might step in and fill the void left by David's exit. Together with the rest of the leadership Barry was learning the challenges associated with better managing the anxiety and fear that had wreaked havoc for so long.

There was one constant theme that surfaced at every Board meeting and in every significant discussion among various Board members. "What does it look like for us to love God and love people as we navigate through the turmoil of the present and begin crafting a new paradigm for our life together moving into the future?" The willingness of the leadership to make that their primary focus brought hope to Barry. For the first time in a long time he felt a sense of optimism returning as he thought about his future and the future of Grenwich.

With the semi-annual congregational meeting drawing closer, the Board turned its attention to the nominating process of selecting and electing new members to fill the various leadership and ministry positions. This would be one of the first opportunities to see whether David Hill had been right in his pronouncement. They were all aware he had confidently predicted that the nominating process would be significantly more difficult given that Barry Moffat was still the Lead Pastor of Grenwich. Barry had his own doubts as to the truth of that pronouncement and others on the Board shared his skepticism. But David's pronouncement and their collective doubts were about to be put to the test.

In the midst of the turmoil Grenwich was experiencing, one of the luxuries they were beginning to enjoy was a growing abundance of people with strong leadership gifts, abilities, and experience. Some of these were people who had been a part of Grenwich for a number of years, while others were a part of the influx of new people who had continued to arrive at Grenwich, choosing it as their place of worship, fellowship, and service. Granted, some had come from other churches, but a number were newcomers to the community having moved in to take up positions of employment in the resource rich region.

As the Nominating Committee began their work, they approached each of the existing Board members to determine their level of interest and willingness to continue serving the people of Grenwich for the upcoming year. All but one indicated a willingness to continue on, in spite of what they had endured so far. Denise Graham, the lone woman on the Board, served notice of her intention to step back from her leadership role on the Board. She indicated that her husband, a well-respected, and very successful businessman in the community had expressed a willingness to let his name stand for nomination should the Committee feel it appropriate. She did not want to create a conflict of interest by both of them being on the Board. Given her husband Chris's credibility and experience as a leader, the Committee was ecstatic to hear the news. There was no question he was a suitable candidate worthy of serious consideration, so they reluctantly accepted her decision, and immediately confirmed Chris's willingness to let his name stand for nomination and election.

Given Chris's openness to involvement on the Board, Brian Ramsay served notice that he would willingly relinquish his role as Interim Chair but remain as a Board member in another capacity. His rationale? Given Chris Graham's experience, credibility, and leadership gifts, he suggested Chris be asked to let his name stand for election as Chair of the Board, something which Chris prayerfully agreed to do. Two additional members were approached to let their names stand, Tom Bishop, a newcomer to the community but a person of solid character, possessing proven leadership gifts, and Linda Booth, a quiet, thoughtful and reflective woman of influence in the congregation. Both agreed to allow their names to stand!

Ironically, in the process there was no arm-twisting, cajoling, guilt manipulation, and no pressuring of any of the individuals who allowed their names to be put forward. What was even more impressive was the calibre of the individuals who would be presented to the congregation for election! This was one of the strongest slate of officers Barry had ever worked with! He went so far as to postulate that this might well be the strongest Board Grenwich had ever elected in their entire history as a church! What made them such a strong Board was not that they were all "Yes" people, or people who automatically supported the pastor. These were people whose Christian commitment was unquestioned. They were people who were willing AND prepared to ask difficult questions of Barry, each other, and the congregation. They were people who were willing to pay the price required in the process of framing a new paradigm for Grenwich. Most importantly, they were people who were committed to lead in a transparent and authentic manner, which was quickly becoming one of the cornerstones of the new paradigm at Grenwich! That in itself was a learning experience for everyone! They were also willing to continue to wrestle with how best they could love God and other people in the context of their leadership roles.

The date of the congregational meeting arrived and surprisingly, there was a larger than average turnout. There were no pressing agenda items to pique the interest of people otherwise not given to attending church business meetings. These kinds of meetings weren't usually high on most people's "bucket list". Perhaps some expected fireworks from David Hill loyalists or a call for a vote of confidence on Barry Moffat's leadership as Lead Pastor, but there were no fireworks and no call for a vote of confidence.

Brian Ramsey conducted an efficient meeting including a report from the Board highlighting the developments of recent months, as well as actions attempted and taken by the Board in an effort to address concerns which had surfaced. The Board was also clear in outlining that moving forward decisions would be handled in a transparent and up-front manner. Questions were raised as to people who had left the congregation, rumoured to have left the congregation, and contemplating leaving the congregation. Again the Board reaffirmed their commitment to visit each individual and/or family who had left with the express purpose of hearing their concerns and offering a prayer of blessing. A report of those visits would be conveyed to the congregation at the next scheduled congregational meeting as a sign of good faith and an expression of the Board's willingness to be held accountable to act in a manner consistent with their stated intentions.

The other significant policy statement emanating from that meeting was the Board's new protocol related to dealing with concerns and conflict within the congregation. Those too would be dealt with in a transparent and up-front manner. The Board would deal with any and all concerns where individuals or groups were prepared to meet face to face with the individual involved, or the leadership. Should they desire it, a member of the Board would be prepared to participate in meetings with individuals, again as an act of transparency and accountability.

When it came time for the election of the new Board, the vote was overwhelming in its support for the new Board. It wasn't, however, unanimous. There were those present who weren't sure they supported the new Board or the approach they were taking to deal with the ongoing concerns which had found expression in David Hill's actions. While they were relatively controlled in their conduct in the meeting, they left committed and more resolved than ever to seek Barry Moffat's ouster. They knew it would not be an easy task.

As the new Board commenced their terms of office, Chris Graham's leadership skills and abilities immediately began to pay dividends. Brian Ramsey had done a great job at stepping in to fill the gap, but his self-acknowledged limitations meant he couldn't provide the kind of leadership Chris could. It didn't mean Brian wasn't a good man, committed to do the right thing. He just did not have the skill set or experience Chris did.

The Board quickly gelled under Chris's leadership and so did the rumours outside of the Board. The most persistent rumours suggested that Barry had successfully surrounded himself with his allies, people who would support him to a fault. What the rumour-mongers either didn't realize or weren't prepared to acknowledge, was that this group of elected leaders were all independent people, clear thinkers who were not afraid of good, honest, and fair debate. They believed they were stronger as a group, and reached better, more God-honouring decisions by having good dialogue and debate. Barry knew he was definitely a better pastor by having a strong Board in place. He wondered aloud if he had died and gone to heaven to be so blessed to have a Board of this calibre. Whatever disagreements they might have within the context of a meeting, they knew that when they left the meeting they did so as members of the same team, pursuing a united and collaborative cause! They had each other's back and they were committed to wrestle with what it meant to do right in loving God and loving people. If they could not set the example as leaders, how could they call others to live out those same values? They were committed to set the example!

In spite of their resolve and commitment, the deeper systemic anxiety refused to abate. There were always individuals willing to fuel and feed it. Several more families indicated their intentions of leaving Grenwich. As promised, the Board followed through on their efforts to arrange meetings with them. Some refused to meet, unwilling to do the harder work of living out what it meant to love one another in the midst of disagreements. Where individuals were willing to meet those meetings were cordial, authentic and open. The Board, in sincere and genuine ways, provided assurances that the door was always open should they wish to return. They always sought permission to pray a blessing over them, encouraging them to find another place of fellowship, worship and ministry. None of these visits were necessarily easy. Who finds enjoyment addressing the kinds of events which led up to these kinds of decisions and meetings? The Board certainly didn't, but they knew they were doing the harder work of framing the new paradigm and no matter how hard it was, no matter the resistance or the honesty of the feedback they received, they were prepared to do what was right! As promised, they reported back to the congregation the results of those meetings. They also provided an update on those who declined an offer to meet.

As the rumours continued to circulate, the Board continued to solicit the input of Larry Harding. Larry suggested that they conduct an open forum meeting following a Sunday morning service. The format would provide people an opportunity to ask whatever questions they wanted, and receive answers from the Board. Larry offered to facilitate the meeting, allowing Board members to more fully participate in the dialogue. The date for the meeting was set and notice was served using every available communication medium. They wanted to ensure that no one could say they were unaware of the meeting or not informed.

The Sunday of the meeting, attendance was higher than usual, with a large number of people new to the church present. Where many might have been excited, Barry cringed. He was afraid. He was afraid that these newcomers might see Grenwich for who they really were, and choose not to stay. He knew some of their "dirty laundry" was probably going to be aired in the course of the meeting, and he couldn't think of a worse meeting for these people to be at! He secretly hoped that many of the new people would not stay for the meeting. His hopes were quickly dashed and his anxiety sky-rocketed when many of the newcomers joined in the meeting!

Larry did an admirable job facilitating the meeting. He provided an overview of the events which had transpired over the preceding months and affirmed his support for the Board and the way in which they had responded to the situation and the resulting turmoil. As expected, some of the David Hill loyalists were present and raised some of the same questions and "anonymous" concerns which had been circulating. They expressed their concerns about people leaving and rumours of people leaving. To each and every question, members of the Board responded in respectful, principled, and transparent ways reaffirming the decisions and commitments they had made earlier. In some cases they were able to provide first-hand updates and information which had been gleaned in the face to face meetings. In other cases they were able to dispel some of the rumours which had been circulating, silencing them in a public forum at least, exposing their lack of substance. The meeting lasted for ninety minutes and for the most part the interactions were cordial, however there was a definite undercurrent and tone present in some of the questions. It seemed evident that some were spokespeople for the ghost of David Hill as well as others who shared his perspective, but were either not present or were unwilling to speak for themselves.

Barry rather hesitantly engaged some of the newcomers following the meeting, apologetic for the fact that they now knew beyond a reasonable doubt that Grenwich was far from perfect as a church. What caught him by surprise was the response he received from many of those who were newer to the church. The recurring refrain was, "It's so refreshing to finally find a church that is willing to have these kinds of conversations in such a transparent and authentic way. We want to be a part of this church! How can we become members?"

To say that Barry was humbled by their response would have been to understate the obvious. Who would have thought that an upheaval the likes of which they were still enduring, would actually serve to draw people to the church? There was no doubt some were leaving, but the ironic reality was that more were coming, and these were people who too shared a deep desire to grow in their understanding and practise of what it meant to love God and love people!

For Reflection and Discussion

1. How has your church dealt with conflict and difficulties in the past? Has it been a positive or a negative experience?

2. What process does your congregation have to ensure you have the most gifted people serving in key leadership positions?

3. How does your congregation deal with people in leadership positions who either don't have the gifts and/or skill set, or who seek to lead motivated more by personal agenda? If you don't have a process to deal with those kind of situations, why do you think that is? What stands in your way of making changes and putting one in place?

4. If the Grenwich Board were to be the elected leadership team in your congregation, how would people respond? Be open to it? Afraid? Resist? Leave the church? Supportive?

Why do you think that is? What does that say about your congregation?

5. If your church was going through a tumultuous time and someone were to suggest a meeting similar to the one facilitated by Larry Harding at Grenwich, what would be the response of people in your congregation? What do you think would characterize the tone or mood of the meeting?

6. To what degree does loving God and loving others shape decision-making in your congregation? Why do you think that is? How could it become more of a factor?

Ken Thiessen

Chapter 11
"Would You Like to Get Well?"

A few years ago CNN ran a commercial where reporter Anderson Cooper was being grilled with a host of relatively obscure questions. As fast as the questions came out of the inquisitor's mouth, the answers rolled off Cooper's lips. After thirty to forty-five seconds of this banter, the inquisitor said to Cooper, "You seem to have a lot of answers," to which Cooper replied, "I'm a reporter!"

If we are honest with ourselves, we have to admit we want answers. Not only do we want answers, we have been trained to give answers. Who ever took a test in school where you received a passing grade for asking a good question? I sure didn't! A passing grade was always dependent on giving the right answer!

The story is told of a final exam for graduating PhD. students. The exam contained one question, "Why?" Students waxed eloquent on this deeply philosophical question. Their graduation depended on getting the right answer. Pages and pages of profound wisdom and insight emanated from this class of astute doctoral students about to reach the pinnacle of academic achievement. All except one student who wrote two words on the piece of paper, walked to the front of the examination hall, handed in his paper and left. The other students were dumbfounded, convinced that this student had just thrown away years of hard work, study, and financial investment!

When the final marks were handed out, the only passing grade went to the student who wrote two words on the exam paper, handed it in, and walked out. The two word answer that resulted in the passing grade? "Why not?" Where others waxed eloquent giving the answer, he raised another question, and passed the test!

Whether or not that is urban legend or an actual occurrence, it illustrates a very important point. We have been conditioned to give answers. On the other hand, questions, especially unanswered questions, stir something really deep in us, often leave us frustrated, propel us on a frantic, even compulsive search for the answers so that life can return to an even keel, or what we feel is an even keel. Unanswered questions cause anxiety to rise within us!

Have you ever noticed that as Jesus interacted with people he wasn't as much about giving answers as he was about posing questions? His questions cut beneath the surface, exposing something deep about the heart of the individual and/or the matter. "What is your name? What do you want? Why do you doubt? Why are you afraid? Who do men say that I am? Who do you say that I am? Where is your faith? Do you believe I can make you see? Do you love me more than these? Who are you looking for? Is this your own question or did others tell you about me? Why are you crying?"

Jesus' questions, at first glance, seem rhetorical; the implied answer obvious and clear. Why are you afraid? I'm gonna die! Why are you crying? My best friend died! What is your name? You know my name! We want answers. Jesus preferred questions. Jesus' questions are questions that no one can answer for you. I can't answer the questions he asks of you and you can't answer the questions he asks of me.

The Encounter With The Paralytic

In John 5 we find the record of Jesus' encounter with a man suffering from a crippling debilitation. Like others who had a variety of infirmities, he spent his time by the waters of the Pool of Bethesda hoping against hope that one day he would be able to dip a toe in the water and experience the mythical healing properties of the water. But alas, day after day his hopes were dashed because no one could help him get close enough to the pool. Someone else was always getting there ahead of him. Who could blame him for not hoping anymore? Who could blame him for quietly resigning himself to spending the rest of his life crippled, paralyzed, and dependent?

Jesus arrived on the scene and posed the most interesting of questions: "Would you like to get well?" "I can't, sir," the sick man said, "for I have no one to help me into the pool when the water is stirred up. While I am trying to get there, someone else always gets in ahead of me." (John 5:6-7)

Try to imagine what life must have been like for this paralytic. John tells us that for 38 years this man had lived with his paralysis. We're not sure how long he had been coming to the Pool of Bethesda hoping somehow to touch the healing waters of the pool and be freed from his paralysis. It's reasonably safe to assume he had been coming for a long time without realizing the result he so desperately wanted.

What might be some of your feelings if that was your life situation, if you were the paralytic in the story of John 5? How do you think you would feel having gone to the pool for so many years, desperately hoping that perhaps this would be the day you might have the chance to walk again and be healed of your paralysis? How would you maintain your sense of hope? Could you maintain a sense of hope? How hard would it be not to throw in the towel and say, "What's the use? I'm destined to be a cripple!"

Jesus' Question And the Paralytic's Response

Into that man's reality, Jesus posed a question, "Would you like to get well?" At first glance, doesn't that seem like an odd question? If you had been paralyzed for 38 years and someone asked you if you would like to get well, how do you think you'd respond? "Duh! Yeah!" But not so quick! Perhaps the question isn't as odd as it appears on the surface. Maybe the answer isn't as obvious as we might first think.

What's at stake for this paralytic as he contemplates his response to Jesus' question? After 38 years, do you think he just might have given up any hope of ever being healed? After 38 years, presumably having exhausted every other available medical option, all to no avail, do you think he might be just a tad skeptical about Jesus' ability to do what others had been unable to do?

I can hear him saying, "Jesus, been there, done that! There were others who were sure they could heal me and look at me! What's the use?" How many times do you think he had allowed himself to hope for healing only to have his hopes dashed? When your hopes are dashed often enough, and for long enough, you give up hope! What if he allowed himself to hope for healing one more time, only to be left with his hopes dashed yet again? It would be easier not to hope because the disappointment would not be as great.

But what if he actually was healed? What then? Life would be very different; he would have to find a job, provide for himself. What would he do? How would he live life as an able bodied person? Commentators suggest that a man like this in that culture would often lose a good living by being cured of his disease.

So Jesus' question was not cruel, stupid, or insensitive. Instead it cut to the core of some deeper issues in this man's life! If you were laying by the pool of Bethesda that day, and Jesus came to you and asked, "Would you like to get well?" how do you think you would respond?

Notice the paralytic's response. "I can't, sir, for I have no one to help me into the pool when the water is stirred up. While I am trying to get there, someone else always gets in ahead of me." He immediately begins to give Jesus all the reasons why he can't be healed, and why he hasn't been healed. But has he really answered the question posed to him? Based on his response, did Jesus have any clearer idea whether or not this man wants healing? Not really! In focusing on his excuses the paralytic avoids giving a straight answer to the question posed by Jesus. Jesus' question required a "Yes" or "No" answer! Okay, maybe an "I'm not sure" or an, "I'd love to be healed but I'm afraid to hope for it!" might have fit too.

What is clear is this man had no clue who he was talking to, a point that comes out later in the story. He didn't realize that the One he is talking to has the power to utter the words and pronounce his healing. Instead he hides behind his excuses, avoiding the real question and the deeper issues surfaced by the question.

The questions that touch the heart are sometimes the hardest ones to answer because they take us beyond our excuses, move us out of the realm of the concrete and the tangible, into the realm of our desires, hopes, and dreams. They move us to those places where our deepest fears and anxieties can no longer be avoided, that place where they are in fact exposed.

Jesus' response is brief and to the point: "Stand up, pick up your sleeping mat, and walk!" That sounds simple enough, doesn't it? But don't rush through the familiarity of the story! Think about what this man was being commanded to do! Would he know how to walk? After 38 years, most of us forget some things. His leg muscles would be significantly weakened from years of inactivity. After 38 years, do you risk doing the unthinkable? Do you risk trying to walk?

The paralytic's response to Jesus' command would reveal his true answer to the "Would you like to get well?" question. Would he hide behind his excuses, or would he stand up, pick up his sleeping mat, and walk? What would you do? What thoughts and feelings would pulsate through you as you contemplated your response?

The paralytic moved beyond his excuses, stood to his feet, picked up his sleeping mat, and his life was forever changed, oblivious to the true identity of the person who had just been the source of his healing. In doing so, he answered the "Would you like to get well?" question. "Yes! I would like to get well!"

The Other Paralytic in the Story

I don't know if you've noticed, but there's another paralytic in the story, and one I think we're prone to overlook because we're so taken in by the faith of the man who's just been healed. We notice all of the other people lying beside the pool waiting for healing as well. But there is actually another group of people that stand in need of healing and in an indirect way the "Would you like to get well?" question is posed to them as well, and awaits a response.

Lurking in the background is a sick system, paralyzed so to speak. It is a system that desperately needs to wrestle with Jesus' question and the implications of it. That system has been sicker for a lot longer than 38 years! It's as if Jesus is asking the leaders of that system to connect the dots by reflecting on the question, "Would you like to get well?"

I suspect that many of us don't tend to think of institutions as having a personality, will, character, temperament, ailments, and the like. But if you stop and think about it, institutions can be healthy or sick, have personality, character, and temperament just like people. In this encounter with the paralytic, we see just such an institution, that of the Jewish religious system as represented in and by the religious leaders.

Their response to the miraculous healing is both shocking and surprising. "So the Jewish leaders began harassing Jesus for breaking the Sabbath rules. But Jesus replied, 'My Father is always working, and so am I'. So the Jewish leaders tried all the harder to find a way to kill him. For he not only broke the Sabbath, he called God his Father, thereby making himself equal with God." (John 5:16-18)

Now if that's not evidence of a sick system desperately needing to wrestle with the "Would you like to get well?" question, I don't know what is! They were the ones who were to lead the way in loving God and loving other people! They were to be the very people who modelled religious devotion and spiritual maturity and yet they were just as sick as the paralytic, perhaps sicker. He was at least aware of his sickness. He recognized his need for healing. They were oblivious to it and in that sense were just as paralyzed, if not more paralyzed! The implied question to them was, "Would you too like to get well?" The Kingdom of God had unmistakably broken into the paralytic's life, the lame made to walk. They were witnesses to it. They knew that the prophets had foretold that this would be one of the signs of the coming Messiah. This was the hope of the Jewish people. There was only one small problem for the religious leaders and that was the Kingdom of God could not break in on the Sabbath! That was indicative of a sick system. Human rules superseded God's plans and design for the Sabbath and humankind. Jesus had come not only to bring physical healing to the paralytic, but spiritual and systemic healing to the Jewish religious system represented and characterized here by the religious leaders. In the process, the religious leaders failed to recognize the presence of the Kingdom in their midst!

Ironically instead of choosing to get well, their plotting to kill Jesus became more focused, intentional, and obsessive, giving an indication of their response to Jesus' question. It was a resounding "No! We're quite fine the way we are! Thank you very much!"

The Anxious Congregation

One of the primary issues an anxious congregation, your congregation, must address is the "Would you like to get well?" question. As much as congregations are often unknowingly held hostage by the anxiety and fear which infect and affect their body life, they are not helpless or powerless to do anything about it! There is hope! There is a way out! But the beginning of the way out is in honestly, transparently, and authentically facing the question posed by Jesus! "Would you like to get well?" REALLY?

The well-known starting point of any journey to greater wholeness is captured in the first few steps of the 12 Steps of Alcoholics Anonymous. While I have amended the steps slightly to the fit the theological paradigm I embrace, the principles fit all too well for any anxious congregation.

Step 1 - We admitted we were powerless; that our lives had become unmanageable.

Step 2 - Came to believe that a power greater than ourselves could restore us to sanity.

Step 3 - Made a decision to turn our will and our lives over to the care of God.

Step 4 - Made a searching and fearless moral inventory of ourselves.

Every person who has struggled with addiction and is now living a life of sobriety knows they are never more than one small step away from returning to the addiction they've been set free from. I recently met a man who had enjoyed 30 years of smoke-free living, having smoked for 27 years previous. What struck me was his "sobering" level of self-awareness. "I'm afraid if I have one cigarette, I won't be able to stop!" You'd think after experiencing 30 years of "sobriety" he'd be free of the urge! But not so!

Anxious congregations are in many ways addicted to their anxiety! It is their drug of choice much like alcohol, drugs, work, sex, tobacco, or food serve to bring comfort to the addict. A person living with an addiction can't imagine living life without their "drug" of choice. Anxious congregations, even if they don't have the level of self-awareness to name their anxiety, can't imagine living life any other way either! Not unlike the paralytic by the Pool of Bethesda, but he at least knew he wasn't "well".

Before we get into the specifics of what it might look like for an anxious congregation to get "well", there are a few additional significant factors that must be identified. Anxious congregations are comprised of anxious individuals. If, as you have been reading, your thoughts have wandered to think about all those "other" people who need to read this book, let me stop you right now. You too are an anxious person who is part of an anxious congregation. Every one of us is guilty, me included! So I am not off the hook and neither are you! Those "other" people may benefit from reading this book, but focus first and foremost on you. Ultimately that is the only person in your world you can control. Most days that is all, if not more than you can handle.

So if there were no anxious people, there would be no anxious congregations! In that sense, you are just as much a part of the problem as those "other" people are! Sorry to be the bearer of bad news. I suspect that news has probably served to cause your anxiety to spike even more! The good news is that if you are a part of the problem, you can now be a part of the solution! But first, "Would you like to get well?" REALLY?

Another key characteristic of anxious congregations is that they are anxious about being anxious, and that only serves to exacerbate the problem! As is the case with the typical addictive family system, they are so anxious about their anxiety that no one feels the freedom to talk about it! That's because in order for someone to even THINK about talking, they would have to first name and own their personal anxiety about the greater systemic anxiety. Are you getting the picture yet? Anxiety really is the gift that keeps on giving, and giving, and giving! It is complex, it is intertwined into the organizational DNA molecules of the congregation, and it functions much like a debilitating virus, threatening a congregation's very existence!

Within an anxious congregation almost everyone intuitively knows the rules in force to keep the lid on the systemic anxiety. The functional purpose for most of the rules is to keep the systemic anxiety in check! The longer an individual has been a part of an anxious congregation, the more intuitive the rules are. Everyone just knows what is acceptable, and more importantly, what is not acceptable, and the less likely they are to notice the presence, impact, and power the anxiety exerts on the whole system! It feels "normal". "It's just the way things are around here."

So as long as nobody enters the system from the outside and actually joins the anxious congregation, the rules persist, unquestioned. It is just easier that way. Life is less anxious for you as an individual if you play by the rules. For most people, the fear of reprisal for breaking the rules, keeps them compliant, maintaining the status quo. That is, until someone like a Barry Moffat arrives on the scene. Then everything changes! Why? People like Barry come in and don't necessarily understand or accept the rules that have been neatly cast in stone like an impenetrable fence governing congregational life. They are not as bound by the fear of the systemic reprisal, or they are willing to move ahead in spite of their fears and their own anxiety. They begin to ask the "Why?" questions. "Why do you do it this way? Why does everyone seem to run from a David Hill? Why don't you do it this way?" In the process what a person like Barry has done is expose the systemic anxiety, and shone a flashlight on the anxiety dust bunnies lurking in the recesses of the congregational system. Poof! The genie has been released from the bottle, and Pandora's box has been opened, for better or for worse! You can't get the genie back in the bottle! You can't slam the lid shut on Pandora's box!

So if the first step to getting "well" is to admit there is a problem, and admit that life has become unmanageable and that you are powerless to do anything about it, then what reasonably minded, genuine, spiritually committed individual or congregation would not want to get well? Who would not want to be free from that?

Before you answer that, do you know anyone who struggles with an addiction and who at present is held captive to it? I suspect you have wondered the same thing about them.

But remember, in the scenario I am laying out here, you're the one struggling with an addiction and you're as much held captive by your anxiety and fear as the next person. So in response to the question I posed, I don't know about you, but I do know about me. Often I wouldn't, and I don't, want to get well! Okay, I lied, I do know about you. You wouldn't, and you don't, either! Neither would your church! Otherwise you would have already done something or done more about it! The hard reality is that as uncomfortable as our anxiety sometimes is, it's the only "normal" we know. So our most apparent options are to do nothing, pretend it doesn't exist, or hold on to what we know, even if we realize that things are not as good as they could be. Or we could actually make the choice to name our anxiety and own it! Take the lid off Pandora's box, so to speak. Usually we opt for the path of least resistance, allowing the anxiety to manage and control us.

The second step requires the humble acknowledgement that we are incapable of "healing" ourselves. Like the paralytic in John 5, we need someone else to help us get to the edge of the pool. We need someone else to help us do what we are incapable of doing for ourselves. But this also means we have to let go of our excuses! The fact that they have worked for so long and served us as a protective security blanket, not unlike Linus in the Peanuts cartoon, letting go is another terrifying part of the process. If we let go of our excuses, what are we left to hold on to? What if nothing changes? What if we are not healed? If we are healed, how will we live life as an "able bodied" and "sober", less anxious person? The very thought of it all leaves us wanting to curl up in a figurative fetal position.

Coming out of that, we know that we will have to "confess our sin" and admit that we have chosen to try to manage life on our own. That can happen most fully as we undertake a "fearless moral inventory" asking God to show us all the ways in which we have failed to fully keep the "greatest commandment" of loving him and loving other people. The more thorough and fearless our moral inventory is, the deeper the confession, and the more profound the potential transformation. What we will discover in this process is that the person we have loved most deeply is the person we see in the mirror! Sometimes we did it knowingly. Most often we did it in ignorance, but we have violated the command nonetheless. Confession is in order.

Following on the heels of confession comes repentance. In some ways, confession is the easy part in that we're agreeing with God that what we have done is wrong. But the test of true confession is the fruit of repentance. Repentance involves changing our habitual ways of managing our anxiety and fear in order to embrace and live out healthier ways of living with, responding to, and managing our anxiety and fear. That will necessitate a change in the way in which we relate to the anxious congregation we are a part of. In some ways we'll be a like a puppy whose eyes have just opened. We will see things differently, notice things that we were unable to see or had failed to see before. We will also have a choice to make. Do we respond according to our old, habitual patterns, or do we choose to discover and develop new patterns which enable us to more fully live out the greatest commandment? How we respond at this particular point in the journey will reveal our answer to the "Would you like to get well?" question. All it takes for an anxious congregation to begin the journey to "getting well" is for one anxious person in that congregation to say emphatically, "Yes, I want to get well!" and then live the fruit of repentance. That's all it takes!!! I can imagine that you have felt that I haven't given much hope to this point in time, but this is the really good news! There is hope. And it can begin with you!

However, there is one important caveat; a "but". We see it illustrated in the healing of the paralytic in John 5 and it has proven itself to be true in countless examples of people struggling with addiction who have made the choice to "get well". Unhealthy systems demonstrate an inherent and obsessive commitment to maintain the status quo. There is a spiritual dynamic and power to that commitment!

Where it would have been quite reasonable and appropriate to expect a celebratory, joyful response from the religious leaders to the healing of the paralytic, we see something quite different! They manifested the kind of obsessive commitment to maintain the status quo which I've just referenced. Their response revealed their own anxiety fuelled by paralysis, their own need for healing, their own defiant response to Jesus' "Would you like to get well?" question!

Countless people who have walked and continue to walk the recovery path from addiction to wholeness could recount the same story. Those who should have been their strongest supporters and cheerleaders actually worked to sabotage the recovery process! I know it sounds incredulous but it is true! Family members and people in the support network actively work to sabotage the addict's path to recovery! The reason? The person struggling with addiction isn't the only one "not well"! They are symptomatic of a system that is unhealthy. Believe it or not, the entire system is much more comfortable with the addict staying "unwell", even dependent on it, than they are committed to getting well!

Here is what it looks like in real life. If we are a part of the same family and you are the addict, then as long as you are sick I can view you as "the problem". I don't need to look in the mirror because you are the one with the "problem". You are the "problem". If you would just get "well" then we would all be fine! That is the reasoning and the logic. So I look at you and avoid looking in the mirror at myself!

Guess what happens when you make the decision to "get well"? As you progress along your path to recovery, you begin to change the way in which you relate to the rest of the system and you change how you relate to me. Suddenly what was predictable becomes unpredictable for you AND for me. Other symptoms begin to emerge, symptoms that before now were masked by your "problem". Therein lies the big wake-up call! I can no longer make you the family scapegoat and the one who is "responsible" for our collective problem! I am forced to look in the mirror. Well, only if I choose to, but it's harder, although not impossible, for me to avoid it.

The same principles hold true in every anxious congregation! There is generally someone who is the identified "problem", a David Hill, if you will. But David Hill is not THE problem. Is he a part of the problem? Absolutely! But so is Barry Moffat! And there is an entire system that encompasses everybody else who is a part of Grenwich that enables a David Hill to continue in his destructive, anxiety induced, "addictive" behaviour. The rest of the system is as anxious as he is. They too are a part of the problem. Their fear keeps them from loving God and loving each other, keeps them from loving David Hill and doing what is ultimately in his best interest. They fail to hold him accountable. That is true for your church too! So we are left to contemplate and reflect on Jesus' question: "Would you like to get well?" REALLY?

For Reflection and Discussion

1. What is your initial reaction having now read this chapter? What struck you the most? Challenged you? Disturbed you? Resonated with you?

2. What are some of the unspoken "rules" which serve to keep the lid on the systemic anxiety in your congregation? In other words, what are the things you either don't talk about or don't do?

3. What has been the response in the past when someone has had the courage to step outside of the system and question or challenge the rules? What are some of the ways in which your congregation maintains the status quo by silencing or marginalizing these individuals?

4. What are the perceived risks to your congregation if someone were to break/challenge the "rules"?

5. If anxious congregations are comprised of anxious individuals, how are you part of the problem? What would be the biggest challenge for you to be a part of the solution by taking conscious steps to "get well"?

6. On a scale of 1 to 10, with 1 being low and 10 being high, how anxious is your congregation?

7. On a scale of 1 to 10, with 1 being low and 10 being high, how willing do you think your congregation is to "get well"? What's holding your congregation back?

Ken Thiessen

Chapter 12
Grenwich - Living into the New Paradigm

As much as Barry felt that Grenwich had turned a corner and begun to wrestle more intentionally with the "Would you like to get well?" question, he wasn't sure he was "enjoying" the journey to greater health and wholeness! Life was filled with lots of uncertainty and unknowns! He was sure of one thing though. Seminary had never prepared him for this, nor had it given him the tools he needed to respond well. Whatever tools he was discovering and developing were coming out of his own sense of being lost at sea, desperately searching for a way to navigate the rough waters of life at Grenwich! In some ways he felt like he was right there in the boat with the disciples on the Sea of Galilee, filled with terror unspeakable, sure that life was quickly ebbing away as the storm raged around them. And Jesus was sound asleep in the midst of it all, apparently oblivious to their fate, insensitive to, and untouched by their anxiety and fear!

Barry's own penchant for learning had taken him down the path of understanding congregations as complex, integrated, and interrelated systems. His journey revealed some interesting, enlightening, and frightening discoveries. He came to realize that anxious congregations demonstrate some predictable and recurring patterns. As he began to view Grenwich through the lens of those predictable and recurring patterns, he didn't like the picture that was emerging of either the church or himself as the pastor. More and more of his anxiety was being exposed for what it was and he was being faced with the "Would you like to get well?" question and at a much deeper level than he had anticipated. He wasn't even sure he really liked the question. He felt so torn. Of course he wanted to get "well" but at the same time he knew there was a price to be paid and he wasn't sure he was prepared to pay that price.

Barry very quickly found himself wanting to make David Hill the focus of his attention and the cause of the turmoil Grenwich was experiencing. Others were as quick to point the finger of blame at David as Barry was, at least those who were more disposed to see things the way Barry and the new Board did. There were others who saw David in the "messianic" role he had occupied for so many years. They were convinced that he was only trying to save the church from sure destruction!

Surprisingly, Barry came to realize that the penchant to find someone or some group on whom to attach responsibility or blame was one of the characteristic patterns of an anxious congregation! Anxious congregations operate on the misguided assumption that if they can just find out who is "responsible" they are halfway to solving the problem! They no longer have to do the hard work of analyzing the problem and addressing the underlying root causes.

Barry began to wonder if he was in fact more anxious than he realized. Was he fuelling the systemic anxiety in ways that weren't healthy or productive? Those questions were haunting for Barry to consider, but as he reflected on them, he realized that he was a significant part of the problem, along with David and others! He wasn't managing his own anxiety in healthy ways and that was having a detrimental effect on

Grenwich's ability to address its present reality in a way that was fundamentally different than the historic pattern.

That realization caught Barry like a left hook out of nowhere. As tempted as he was some days to pack it in, resign his position at Grenwich and move to another church, this newfound awareness stopped him dead in his tracks. He realized that if he thought moving to another church was going to solve the problem and be fundamentally different, he was fooling himself. People are people no matter where you go. David Hill might not be at the next church, but he was confident there would be a David Hill type of person there. The issues might be different but the dynamics would be similar. There would be plenty of anxious people in that congregation as well, feeding, fuelling, and supporting the collective anxiety! More importantly, if all Barry did was bail out on the challenging situation at Grenwich and move to another church, he would bring with him his own anxiety and add his contribution to the mix in his new ministry setting and do so in ways that were also unhelpful and unhealthy.

What became quickly apparent to Barry was that running was not a reasonable, positive, or acceptable option. Nor was it God-honouring. He also didn't believe it was the best way he could live out his commitment to love God and love people. If he was going to do the hard work of answering the "Would you like to get well?" question, he had best do it in the context of Grenwich, together with the people and the leadership of Grenwich. If loving God and loving people meant anything at all, if it really was the greatest commandment he was committed to live out, then perhaps Grenwich was the venue to put it to the test, continuing to learn what it meant to live it out and do it well! He knew how fortunate he was to have a leadership team who shared a similar commitment and were prepared to work hand in hand with him in this process.

Several of them had already verbalized their fear that he might leave and encouraged him not to run! They wanted him to stick around and lead them through to the other side, whatever that looked like.

In spite of the fact David Hill had physically left Grenwich, the dynamics which enabled him to exercise his hold on congregational life for so many years were still very present! What Barry found somewhat surprising was that others were stepping in to fill the void left by David's exit and were taking on the role David had occupied. While they, or David for that matter, would never have described their mission as having a messianic urgency to it, it was abundantly clear they felt that should they not continue on with the cause, Grenwich was doomed to obscurity with only tattered ruins remaining if Barry Moffat was not removed as Lead Pastor and David Hill reinstated as Chair of the Board.

What Barry realized as the saga continued to unfold was that the unhealthiest of organizational systems have a strange co-dependency that necessitates all of the defined "roles" being filled. Should a vacancy exist or emerge, intuitively, impulsively, someone else in the system rushes to fill the void, and Grenwich was no exception. As much as some thought the solution to the current crisis lay in Barry Moffat leaving, others were convinced that since David Hill was no longer there, they had turned the corner and the crisis was over. Both were wrong!

Barry realized that the problem in an anxious congregation, Grenwich Anxious Community Church, was always bigger than one individual. While there are individuals whose personality and behaviours exert more influence on the system, the problem is always greater than the individual. Neither removing Barry Moffat or David Hill, or both for that matter, would significantly and automatically move the system to greater health. The problems ran much deeper. While this was enlightening for Barry, it wasn't necessarily comforting. It meant there was much more work to do.

The one void at Grenwich that wasn't being filled was the financial void. The absence of David's ongoing support of the ministry at Grenwich was noticeable. As Barry and the leadership talked about the ongoing financial situation, they kept coming back to the point that in a real sense, David's financial support of the church was tainted because there were always strings attached. The money kept flowing as long as Grenwich did what David wanted. When they didn't, the money supply slowly dried up. The leadership were no longer prepared to accept that as normative behaviour. They were in essence saying "No" to David Hill and anyone else who thought their money was going to dictate and control what happened at Grenwich. The leadership believed that while the challenges, financial and otherwise, of the present were real, God would honour their efforts to do the right thing, even if it involved some pain along the way! They were committed and willing to pay the price.

Perhaps most surprising to Barry and the leadership was the continued presence of new people at weekend worship services. Without exception, each week there were new faces, sometimes people from other churches, and sometimes people who were new to the community, in the midst of, and in spite of, the turmoil and upheaval! While new people were coming, there was still an exodus of others although that exodus was starting to wane. The one thing that began to emerge was a new attitude towards those who felt the need to leave. There was a decreasing sense that those individuals were the "problem", less of a sense of relief, and a growing sadness at the loss that many felt.

The Anxious Congregation

But in this somewhat odd and conflicted reality another characteristic of anxious congregations was emerging. Anxious congregations have a way of attracting other highly anxious people. This is particularly true in congregations where the level of denial or lack of awareness as to the extent of the anxiety is high. Anxious people intuitively know where the dynamics are fertile for them to continue to offer their "gift". Conversely, as anxious congregations are able to begin to name and own their collective anxiety, and move towards healthier ways of managing it, they begin to attract other like-minded individuals. Gradually the chronically anxious realize there is less room for them and their anxiety to function unchallenged and unaddressed. Those people tend to move on to other contexts where they can live life in a more "normal" way, at least how they define "normal".

Barry began to see this dynamic manifest itself in life at Grenwich and it gave some sense of meaning and explanation to what was taking place. At the same time, he realized there was no reason to be glib or smug. They needed to maintain a heightened sense of vigilance in naming and managing their individual and collective anxiety and fear if they were to see long term, substantive change. That remained the ultimate goal.

As Barry became more attuned to dynamics at Grenwich he began to notice that there were some people whom he described as "busy-bodies". They were the people who were always first to say "Yes" to volunteering, even when no one was asking for volunteers! These were the people who took on far more roles in the church than was good for them or others. On the surface they seemed to be motivated by a deep concern for the church but as Barry observed them, he began to notice some patterns. They volunteered for things irrespective of whether or not they had the gifts or skill set required for the task. Sometimes they volunteered without even being asked! Most other people would affirm them in their efforts, even when it was clear they were not suited for the task or the role. Oddly, the more these people "stepped up to the plate" the more others sat on the sidelines. At the end of the day everyone knew that "Martha" would do it. While these people appeared to have servant hearts, what Barry noticed was an angry, bitter undertone that would occasionally slip out. He also noticed they were extremely resistant to the involvement and input of others. When other, more gifted people offered to get involved or provided suggestions as to how things could be done more efficiently or effectively, there was an angry resistance and a possessive territorialism that surfaced. Occasionally they would threaten to "resign" if they did not get their way. In this sense they were using their "ministry" to hold the church hostage.

One particular individual seemed to have a knack for this, more so than anyone else. Frank had been a dedicated and very gifted volunteer responsible for much of the maintenance in the church building. While he appeared pleasant and cooperative much of the time, when he would report to the Board he did so with an attitude and an edge. On more than one occasion he had tendered his resignation and under David Hill's leadership the Board had always cajoled and coaxed him to continue on, reassuring him of his value to the congregation. In many respects they were right because Frank did bring a lot to the congregation.

With David Hill's resignation as chair of the Board, and the resulting leadership transition, one of the unanswered questions was how this would affect Frank's demeanour when providing his regular reports. At one of the early meetings of the new Board, Frank again indicated he was contemplating resigning. True to form the Board responded in classic fashion, cajoling and coaxing him to reconsider, just as David Hill before them had done. Frank relented, the status quo firmly intact.

Several months later, Frank again tendered his resignation. The Board, having had opportunity to observe more of Frank's behaviour and also learn more about the way in which anxiety was unduly exerting influence on the decision-making process at Grenwich, decided to accept his resignation. No cajoling, no coaxing, just expressions of appreciation for Frank's years of faithful service. What they were not prepared for was the angry outburst from Frank, the depth of which they had never observed before! He was livid! What quickly became apparent was that Frank was using his resignation as a manipulative ploy to get his way. The minute the Board accepted his resignation, his plan were thwarted and his deeper motivations exposed! He lashed out at them accusing them of not appreciating all he had done for the church, suggesting they had done the same thing to David Hill, and others who had left. None of the Board members bit the bait that was laid for them. They simply allowed Frank to vent. They reasoned that since he was a fifty-something adult, he was also fully capable of making adult decisions and living with the consequences and they were fully prepared to respect that. When Frank finished his rant, Chris Graham very calmly but firmly reaffirmed the Board's appreciation for all that Frank had brought to the position, indicated they would respect his decision and accept his resignation. In that moment, the Board broke one of the unhealthy patterns characteristic of anxious congregations and served notice that others would not be permitted to use their "ministry" to hold the congregation hostage.

Coming out of that meeting, the Board made another important decision to revisit their process of recruiting people for ministry involvement. They realized there were other people involved in ministry who should not be involved, at least not in the areas they were currently serving. The reason being, their gifts and skill set better suited them to serve in other capacities. There were others who were very gifted sitting passively on the sidelines. The Board believed that a part of what it meant to love God and love people was to help people discern their ministry gifts and then match those gifts with a suitable ministry position. In some cases this would require them to redirect individuals to another ministry area. This had the potential to be a difficult process depending on how the individual responded. In other situations it would involve extending an invitation or a challenge to someone sitting on the sidelines, encouraging them to "get in the game" and use their gifts to help the congregation grow. The Board agreed this was something they needed to work towards so they began to put in place an implementation plan.

As Barry continued to reflect on the transformation that was taking place, he was encouraged and felt a growing sense of hope. What disturbed him was the way in which the tone of the attacks by those loyal to David Hill was becoming more underhanded, vicious, and personal. The majority of the attacks were directed at Barry and they were relentless. Barry and Diane were beginning to feel the weight of those attacks and it was getting more difficult to shield their kids from what had been swirling around them for quite some time now. Barry was having serious second thoughts as to whether or not he should resign and move on. Individually he sat down with Chris Graham, Randy Mann, and Tom Bishop, Board members he trusted, men he knew would tell him what he needed to hear, not just what he wanted to hear. These were principled leaders who had demonstrated their willingness to pay the price to see Grenwich more effectively name and manage its anxiety and grow in their love for God and one another. As Barry met with them individually he asked them each the same question: "Am I so much a part of the problem that I can no longer be a part of the solution?" He knew he would get a straight answer from each of them, even if it was hard for them to do. What surprised him was that each of them responded with an emphatic "No!" Each reassured Barry that he was not the problem. Moreover, each of them suggested that what Grenwich most needed at this point in its journey was someone with Barry's leadership gifts and abilities to continue to lead them through this significant period of turmoil and transition. Each of them expressed a deep desire that Barry stay around long enough to see some of the fruit of his labours. Reassured by their support, Barry pledged to continue to lead but again stated his need for their ongoing feedback, input, and collaboration as they grew in their understanding of what living into the new paradigm really meant.

As the Board continued to meet, a new and interesting dynamic began to manifest itself, an indication of an increasing measure of health and an ability to more effectively manage the systemic anxiety. Where once Board meetings used to be characterized by tacit compliance and agreement, now Board meetings were engaging with good debate, discussion, and dialogue. This was a new experience in that the Board had never experienced this kind of open, frank conversation before, at least not where everyone felt the freedom to be honest and frank! In the past, it had usually been only David Hill who felt the freedom, and everyone else quietly nodded in agreement, whether they really agreed or not. What was even more refreshing about the current developing pattern was that even though there was healthy debate, it rarely became personal. It was more about the deeper issues and rarely about a person's perspective on the issue. When the Board left the confines of the Board room, they did so with the understanding that they were all on the same team and they had each other's back! There would be no entertaining or advocating a contrary message outside the Board room. Barry felt a new-found freedom and support. He knew that collectively they would reach better decisions because of their ability to respectfully debate and dialogue together. He also knew he would be a better pastor for it! He was becoming more convinced that anxious congregations experiencing anxious times have the most hope of moving forward in positive ways if and when there are strong leaders in place, leaders who are better able to manage their own anxiety even as they seek to lead from the eye of the storm! Barry was beginning to live that experience!

For Reflection and Discussion

1. Where have you seen blaming and scapegoating manifested in your congregation? How has that "helped" your congregation to manage the collective anxiety and fear?

2. Who are the people you see as the "problem" in your congregation? What if the problem is bigger than one individual or group? What are the implications for you? For your congregation?

3. Do you have someone like Frank in your congregation? How have people responded when this person has threatened to resign?

4. Who are the "busy-bodies" in your congregation? Why do you think others sit back and allow them to continue to serve in areas where they might not be gifted? Has anyone

ever tried to challenge them? If so, what have been the results?

5. If these are some of the characteristics of anxious congregations, what might be some of the implications for how you recruit people for various ministry and leadership positions?

Ken Thiessen

Chapter 13
The Change Process - Risk and Learning; Faith and Courage!

As you are beginning to see, anxiety exerts a much more powerful influence on your congregation than what you have realized or acknowledged! It is pervasive with some predictable manifestations and patterns, and it has a throttling grip on many a church, perhaps yours! I am sure that in one way or another, you can relate to some of the experiences of Grenwich. You've probably found yourself identifying with some of the characters, perhaps naming the David Hill in your own congregation. I would not be surprised if some of you have regrets about accepting my invitation to this journey.

The old adage, "ignorance is bliss!' is so true. Don't ever let anyone tell you otherwise and if they do, assume they are probably a chronically anxious person. There is something so appealing about ignorance! When life has been particularly challenging or difficult, haven't you wished you could return to the simplicity of life as a child? When you were a child someone else did all of the worrying for you, took care of all your needs. You were much freer to experience life as it happened, without a care in the world! There is something so appropriate about that when you observe it in a toddler, but so inappropriate when you observe or experience an adult or a group of adults living life that way.

When you strip away the veneer of an anxious congregation, that is what you discover. Sadly, as many of us live life in the context of anxious local congregations, we do so as children, clinging tightly to our naive ignorance, bound by our fears. When someone attempts to challenge and expose our ignorance and call us to face our fears, we start kicking, screaming, and stomping our feet at those who are calling us to leave behind our childish ways and more fully engage life as responsible, mature adults. We are much more content to run around as adults wearing our disposable diapers sucking on our overgrown pacifiers! While the imagery is repulsive, and should be, sadly all too often it could be used to describe an anxious congregation.

Robert Quinn, in his book *Deep Change*, speaks powerfully regarding the challenges associated with deep, systemic change. He says, "The land of excellence is safely guarded from unworthy intruders. At the gates stand two fearsome sentries – risk and learning. The keys to entrance are faith and courage."[5] While Quinn is not addressing a church context per se, he understands the dynamics of the change process in any organization or individual. He has very succinctly identified some of the key challenges for an anxious congregation if it is going to begin the process of exchanging old, comfortable, albeit unhealthy habits for new, sometimes frightening, more mature, and God-honouring relational patterns.

For an anxious congregation to begin the process of deep change, what is required is a willingness to risk engaging the anxiety and fear, allowing all of the associated feelings to rise to the surface, experiencing them in all of their fullness, and

---

[5] Robert E. Quinn, Deep Change: Discovering the Leader Within. (San Francisco, CA: John Wiley & Sons Canada, Ltd., 1996), 163

sometimes fury. In the process they will discover that there is life in the midst of, and beyond the anxiety and fear.

My wife Bev required bi-lateral knee replacement surgery because both of her knees had exceeded their "best before" date. She was "privileged" to have an orthopaedic surgeon who would replace both knees in the same surgical procedure! If you have ever had any kind of joint replacement surgery, I know what you are thinking: "What doctor in his right mind would ever suggest that and who would be crazy enough to go through with that?" You would not be alone because my wife said that too! But as she listened to the advice of her surgeon, checked his credentials (he was the chief orthopaedic surgeon for a Canadian professional football team), talked with others who had undergone knee replacement, she decided to face her fears and the associated risks, and take the plunge!

The day of surgery her surgeon gave her the option of changing her mind. She instructed him to do both knees at the same time and signed the necessary medical release documentation. His most compassionate words of comfort to her were, "Tomorrow you will think this is the dumbest decision you've ever made, but you'll get over it! All of my patients do." He was genuine, sincere, and authentic but if his goal was to provide comfort to an anxious patient, he probably could have used other words which would have been more effective. Mustering up my most comforting and sensitive skills I assured her, "He is a very good doctor!" The truth isn't necessarily comforting!

Guess what? The next day, when Bev literally did not have a good leg to stand on and she was being "encouraged" to try walking with the aid of parallel bars, she fully agreed that this was the dumbest decision she had ever made! When she saw her surgeon for a post-op appointment five weeks later he asked her, "So, are you glad you did it?" Without hesitation she responded with a resounding, "Yes! Why would I want to go through this twice?" He responded, "That's what they all say!" Today, five months later as she walks the sandy beaches on the shore of Banderas Bay, she is more certain than ever she did the right thing. Make no mistake about it; there were days along the way where she had serious doubts and questions as she was doing the hard work of physiotherapy.

The process of a local church embarking on the journey to deep change involves some similar kinds of thoughts and feelings. In some ways I am the surgeon giving you the options, outlining the associated risks. In as compassionate a way as possible (oh, and by the way, mercy gifts are not my strongest suit which my wife will attest to) I'm telling you that the day after your decision you are going to wake up thinking you have made the biggest mistake in your life. Then I'm following that up by telling you, "This too shall pass!" Seriously, that is probably what it is going to feel like, but I can assure you, with as much mercy and compassion as I can muster, once you get down the road a ways and gain some perspective, you will not regret it! At least not all the time!

One of the realities in joint replacement surgery, particular knee replacement, is a heightened risk of blood clots forming in the legs. Untreated, they can be fatal. That is a risk which can be managed, but it is real none the less. As you and your congregation embark on the journey to deep change, there are associated risks. Things will get worse before they get better! That's not just a risk; that will be your reality. Not everyone will buy in to the process. Some will cling tenaciously to their overgrown pacifier and will throw the biggest adult-sized toddler temper tantrum you can imagine (and then some). That is a risk. Some people may abandon ship and leave your congregation. Nasty things might be said about and to those who are seen as the instigators of the change! Probably most of it will be spoken "about" rather than directly "to" those deemed "responsible". That is the preferred modus operandi of chronically anxious people! Those risks are real. Acknowledge your fear of the risks and the associated pain, and embark on the journey anyway!

As my wife began her rehab process, she made a surprising recovery. Because her knees were in such a deteriorated state, she was "crooked" (her doctor's words not mine). This affected her gait and unbeknownst to her, she had developed some significant compensatory behaviour. Now, with two new knee joints, her legs were straight and she literally had to learn how to walk all over again! In the process she started using muscles she had not used in years, at least not in the way they were being required now that she had new knees and was once again "straight".

Her physiotherapy routine was painful. No matter how much she prepared herself for that mentally, it was quite another thing to experience it firsthand, to feel the tendons, ligaments, and muscles as they attempted to recuperate from the trauma induced by the surgery. Without going into all of the gory details as to what transpires in knee replacement surgery, those parts of the body's anatomy were traumatized! There is no gentler way to describe it.

In her preparation for surgery, the recurring message she was given by health care professionals and others who had undergone knee replacement surgery was, "Whatever else you do post-op, do your physio! When in doubt, do your physio!" They even had her begin an exercise routine before surgery! We know individuals who've had knee replacement surgery, who, because of the pain of rehab have chosen not to be disciplined in their post-op physiotherapy routine, and they will forever bear the consequences for their decision. And they had only endure one knee replacement, not two.

In spite of the pain, Bev was disciplined in her physiotherapy routine. One other small detail to keep in mind was that I was her primary caregiver and rehab "coach". Before surgery this was one of her greatest concerns. She knew herself, and me, pretty well. Thirty plus years of marriage gives you some insights about each other that most everyone else doesn't possess! She knows that I am a task-oriented, Nike "Just Do It" kind of a person. She has a pain tolerance level that she would describe as low. When I suggest that might be a generous assessment, she reminds me she gave birth to our two children and that usually ends the discussion. She was concerned as to whether our marriage could survive the rehab! My question to her was, "Do you really think this is the most difficult thing that we will experience together?" Her immediate response was, "Yes!" Well, we're through that process, we're still married and we still want to be married!

For the anxious congregation that has made the decision to begin the process of naming the collective anxiety and managing the fear in new, healthier ways, I would suggest the process you are going to engage will feel pretty similar to what I have just described and you'll experience some similar dynamics.

I am telling you right up front, that your path to a healthier experience of congregational life is going to require discipline, relational rehab if you will. You will need to be disciplined as you begin that process, because like my wife prior to her surgery, you are "crooked". There are relational muscles that are so used to being "crooked" that they are going to have something to say as you try to get "straight"! The relational muscles are going to be traumatized in the process of rehab. It is going to hurt; you are going to want to give in and give up.

Those muscles will always have names and faces attached to them because they are real live people! In their own way they will each be screaming, "STOP!!" Sometimes the names and faces will surprise you. You will not expect them to react quite the way they do. Occasionally the face that will surprise you the most is the one you see in the mirror. You will be the one wanting to pack it in, because the cost of rehab feels too great!

Let me give you a word of encouragement; don't stop. Do your physio, do your physio, do your physio. When in doubt, do your physio! It will hurt in the short term, but it will be worth it in the long run! Trust me! Bev was told she would require the aid of a walker for at least 6 weeks following surgery. She would then gradually move to two crutches, then one crutch and eventually, at approximately three months, a cane. Three weeks post-op she was starting to move much better so I casually suggested she try walking with crutches. I thought she was going to hit me with a crutch given the look I got! Our daughter and son-in-law were home so she restrained herself. You know that routine if you've got married kids. You try harder to behave yourselves as couples when they're around, and some days you actually succeed! She took the crutches and started using them on a Friday evening. On Sunday, just two days later, our son-in-law said to her, "You're walking a lot quicker already!" Two days! At six weeks she went from two crutches to one crutch and at approximately eight weeks she graduated to a cane, a metallic copper one with lots of bling; a true fashion accessory! It came complete with a retractable ice pick, a valuable addition given Canadian prairie winters!

So why? Why was she able to see an accelerated recovery? Before you think of causing me bodily harm, hear me out! The "Why?" is a legitimate question. She was willing to undergo the surgical procedure knowing all the risks, and in spite of the risks. She knew there would be pain, but she was already living with pain. She was afraid, and I mean she was AFRAID! She will readily acknowledge that herself. She was afraid of the risks, the pain, the post-op physio, the pain, the rehab, the pain... Who could blame her? I sure wasn't going to, but I did try to coach her through that process and I think she would say most days I succeeded. Had her fears, or the risks paralyzed her, and had she been unwilling to learn new ways to manage pain and learn to walk all over again (literally without a leg to stand on), this part of the book would read very differently and so would her experience!

For an anxious congregation, your congregation, the decisions you make related to the risks, or what feels like risks, associated with getting well, and the degree to which you are willing to learn new ways of managing the anxiety and the fear, will determine whether or not you ever experience greater health. In some ways it's like learning new dance steps as you walk forward together. How you engage that process will determine the degree to which you experience greater health. My advice? Do the physio!

So what was the key for Bev in her rehab process? Well if the two sentries that carefully guard the door to excellence are risk and learning as Robert Quinn suggests, then the keys to entrance are faith and courage. Bev demonstrated a lot of faith in the process. If you were to ask her, she might question how much faith she really had but in all seriousness, she trusted the advice of her doctor, she trusted his medical competence and his reputation. She knew that she was very fortunate to have the opportunity to be on his surgical wait list. In that sense she knew she was in very good hands. She trusted others who had undergone the same surgery who encouraged her along the way to go through with it. She trusted the nursing staff and physical therapists who worked with her in her rehab.

Most importantly, she believed that God had put the pieces together in a way that resulted in her surgery being moved up by six months, something which came as a complete and unexpected surprise! After processing all the data, she chose to believe and to act on that belief!

Did she ever have doubts? Of course she did! There were days when she did the "I'm gonna do this. No I'm not! Am I crazy? Yes I am!" routine. On those days it was the faith of some of those close to her that got her through. On the day after surgery when they got her up to walk and she walked eight feet with the aid of parallel bars, she BELIEVED! Later that same day when the medical staff attempted to get her up for her second round of physio and she fainted, unable to go through with it, she lost faith and blamed herself for "failing". Blood loss during surgery, morphine, and the effects of general anaesthetics will do that to you. Your sense of equilibrium is affected! But slowly each day she continued to believe, some days with faith the size of a mustard seed, but she continued none the less.

Each and every day through the rehab journey she demonstrated levels of courage which caused others to look on in admiration and amazement! Each patient in the orthopaedic ward of the hospital was required to put identification markings on their walker. Bev's was a luggage tag with a picture; a picture of the two of us walking the beaches on Banderas Bay. That was her motivation! She was going to walk the beaches again in five short months and she was DETERMINED!!! So on those days when the resolve to risk and learn were low, when faith and courage were in shorter supply than what she wanted or needed, she'd take a look at that luggage tag, she'd resolve again to do the rehab, and she'd muster up the courage to try it one more time! She never gave up! I didn't say she didn't feel like giving up. But she never did! The memories evoked by the picture on the luggage tag have been our reality again, five months post-op!

Some days Bev still wonders whether she's really making good progress or progressing as quickly as she should. On those days, God has a way of sending other people who've either been through knee replacement surgery or who work in orthopaedic medicine to encourage her. More than once she had people who "know" knee replacement surgery and rehab express positive shock and amazement at the speed and quality of her recovery. After spending almost 10 hours walking the markets and the beaches of Puerto Vallarta a good friend said to her, "You could never have done last year what you have done today!" Bev gave a somewhat shocked response of, "Really?" She had forgotten how bad it was before. On days when she feels like she's not making as much progress as fast as she would like, that's when she realizes again the importance of having others to support and encourage her on the journey, helping give her perspective.

Faith and courage are the same keys required to get past the sentries of risk and learning in the anxious congregation. Faith, first of all, that God calls you to address your anxiety in ways that move you to greater health. Faith that when (not if) God calls you to do that, he is also going to give you everything you need to safely arrive at your destination! Faith that what seem like risks to you are really no risks to God! Faith that God would not lead you down a path that would ultimately harm you and your congregation. His motivation is loving and he has your best interests in mind! He wants what is best for you. Faith that on those days when it's hard for you to muster up faith of your own, he will carry you on the faith of others.

It will require courage. The way forward will feel scary, and fraught with danger, and it will require discipline, persistence, and hard work. That applies to individuals within the anxious congregation and it applies to the collective of individuals who comprise the anxious congregation. Personally, some days you won't feel like you have what it takes to continue on because your faith and courage will be weak. You will need others to help you muster up your faith and courage to keep going. Other days you will be the one encouraging and supporting others along the way, reassuring them that they have what it takes to stay in the game, to keep on the journey. In the end it will be worth it!

For Reflection and Discussion

1. On a scale of 1 - 10 (1 being low, 10 being high), how would you rate your congregation's willingness to risk and learn? How would you rate yourself personally?

2. On a scale of 1 - 10 (1 being low, 10 being high), how would you rate your congregation's demonstration of faith and courage? How would you rate yourself personally?

3. Who are the risk-takers in your congregation? How does your congregation typically respond to them?

4. Who are the courageous people of faith in your congregation calling you to step out even if/when it feels risky and scary? How does your congregation typically respond to them?

5. If Jesus' "follow me" call always involves risk and learning, and requires courage and faith, what does your congregation's historic pattern indicate about your practical willingness to respond to that call? Why do you think that is? What's holding you back?

Chapter 14
The Anxious Congregation Rehab Regimen

If the change process involves risk and learning, faith and courage, then what might a rehab regimen look like in the context of an anxious congregation? What relational and organizational muscles might need to be worked, stretched, strengthened, or toned in order to facilitate healthy progress to a "new normal"? How many people really need to engage this regimen in order for an anxious congregation to make significant positive and healthy movement?

Let me answer the last question first - ONE! I wouldn't be surprised if that generates a puzzled, questioning look of disbelief. I also wouldn't be surprised if at least one neck has been dislocated and whiplashed from the shock! But hear me out. One person committed to "get well" can bring about deep, systemic change to an entire anxious congregation! Think back to Grenwich for a moment. What started the ball rolling? It was Barry Moffat's willingness and ability to name and manage his own anxiety and fear in a healthier way which gave Grenwich the opportunity to move together towards greater health as a congregation.

Barry was able to step back and take a look at the bigger picture. It's almost as if he had an out of body experience. Not only was he able to see the bigger picture, he was able to see his part in the bigger picture, for better and for worse!

What's true about every relational system is that each individual within a given system contributes to the healthy AND unhealthy functioning of that system. In that sense, everyone is guilty! That's a significant realization Barry came to as he took a step back and observed the big picture. He realized that he was a part of the problem, but he also realized he could be a catalytic contributor to the solution.

You know that anxious congregation you're a part of? Guess what? You do something to either raise the anxiety, enable the anxiety, perpetuate the anxiety, or cause the anxiety! I don't suspect you'll have any problem accepting responsibility for the ways in which you contribute to the healthier functioning of that anxious congregation, but you might chafe a bit at the realization that you are in some way responsible for the unhealthy functioning! You may not be aware of exactly how you do that, but assume that you in some way contribute to the problem. In this case, ignorance may be bliss, but it doesn't let you off the hook!

The other important thing that Barry was able to do early on in the process was to remain engaged with the system he knew as Grenwich Community Church. Oftentimes when you step back and take a look at the bigger picture you don't like what you see. There are several common temptations at this point in the journey. One is the temptation to turn and run! Who needs this? Why should I stick around! Another is to begin to identify the people whom you think are "responsible" or the "problem". Usually that's not a complicated process because you're quickly able to identify the people who you least connect with, or who grate on you the most. It's easy to identify them as the "problem".

Another common temptation is to complain to someone else about the "problem" and in that sense you have just given your gift of anxiety to someone else in the system. If they really love you they'll turn it back to you and say something like, "What would you like to do about that?" More often than not they'll take the bait you've set for them and before you know it the hook has gone so far down it's next to impossible to safely extract it! Just because these temptations are common doesn't make them right! So what if "everybody's doing it"? It still fails the "love God and other people" test!

In my experience there aren't many people like Barry Moffat. They're an uncommon and rare breed. But I do encounter them, and when I do I know they're people who have tangibly demonstrated their willingness to risk and learn, and I intuitively know they are people of great faith and courage! These are people to be admired. These are people who possess an abundant capacity to mentor others! These are people worth following! They're also catalytic change agents! They're not perfect people, but the one thing I know about them is this: they're relentless in their own efforts to more fully understand what it means to love God and love other people and to live that out, no matter what the cost!

There's another thing that I often notice when I meet people like a Barry Moffat. As they embark on their journey of relating differently to the anxious congregation they're a part of, they often do so feeling a profound sense of loneliness, convinced they're the only one who feels the way they do. They're afraid because they're embarking on a journey into the vast unknown, but they go there anyway! They refuse to allow their anxiety and fears to immobilize them. They refuse to use them as an excuse. As their relational patterns change, they begin to name some of the ways in which anxiety manifests itself in the congregation. As time goes on someone else in that same anxious congregation will timidly approach a Barry and say almost under their breath, "Can I talk to you?" What ensues is most fascinating. Almost without exception, the confession of the timid, "anxious" inquirer is that they too share some of the same thoughts, feelings, and perceptions that a Barry does. They too share the sense of loneliness, convinced they are the only one! Quickly they form their own informal support group and together they talk about what it means to love God and other people, adapt and modify the ways in which they relate to the rest of the anxious congregation, and slowly others join them on the journey!

All it takes to bring about meaningful, substantive change to an anxious congregation is ONE self-differentiated individual willing to pay the price of changing the way in which he or she relates with and to the anxious congregation! That's it! It involves risk and learning, faith and courage. It's really about the power of one! One person can make a significant, positive impact! The bigger question is this: Now that you're aware and informed, will you be the one?

Before you answer that, allow me to outline some of the common patterns which regularly present themselves in anxious congregations, anxious businesses, anxious nonprofit organizations, anxious denominations, and anxious families!

The Blame Game

One of the most pronounced manifestations of anxiety in any organization is what I call the blame game. Anxious congregations are obsessive in their efforts to find someone to blame, someone on whom to cast responsibility. This pattern is not new or unique. From the beginning of recorded time, the blame game has been one of the pastimes of choice. Adam blamed Eve. Eve blamed the serpent. Cain blamed Abel. Moses blamed the children of Israel. Someone blamed you. You blamed someone else.

The Anxious Congregation

The concept is also firmly rooted in Israel's religious traditions. As a part of the Day of Atonement, Aaron was instructed to present a live goat and lay both of his hands on the head of the goat. In that symbolic gesture, the sins of the people were transferred to the head of the goat and then a man specially chosen for the task was charged with driving the goat into the wilderness. (Leviticus 16:20-22) Thus the term scapegoat!

Anxious congregations are obsessed with casting blame and identifying a scapegoat in an unhealthy attempt to manage the collective anxiety. Wherever and whenever you find a relational system characterized by blaming and scapegoating, assume that you're dealing with a highly anxious system! Dan Allender suggests, "The greater the crisis, the more we will want to find someone to blame."[6] Most often the *perceived* nature and urgency of the crisis will have been exaggerated by a highly anxious person or group, but the propensity to blame will beat like a heart racing out of control! In reality, the crisis is rarely as urgent as it's been painted out to be.

What functional purpose does blaming and scapegoating serve in the context of the anxious congregation? How does it help manage the collective anxiety? It allows others within the system to ignore their complicity in the overall problem. In identifying the "source" of the problem, there is an underlying, and sometimes stated belief that the problem is halfway to being resolved. If I'm a part of an anxious congregation and I've identified you as the "problem" then the solution is for you to "get your act together and mend your ways!" You're the problem! You're the one who has to change! My index finger is pointed squarely at you, and probably so are a whole bunch of others! "In organizations

---

[6] Dan B. Allender, Leading With a Limp. Turning Your Struggles Into Strengths. (Colorado Springs, CO: Waterbrook Press, 2006), 64

where anxiety is often expressed in blame, to avoid being blamed becomes a constant preoccupation."[7] "Once a scapegoat has been found, all further thinking about the situation is suspended."[8] In other words, my mind's already made up so don't confuse me with the facts! Using dramatic imagery, Jeffrey Miller says, "Once an anxious organization resorts to 'human sacrifice,' chronic anxiety increases as survivors secretly fear their turn is coming."[9] That's a pretty graphic way of describing the relational dynamics in an anxious congregation but it's not far from the truth or reality!

It's important to be clear about one thing here. In identifying blame as an unhealthy manifestation of systemic anxiety, I'm not talking about a lack of accountability or saying accountability isn't important. In an anxious congregation, the rules are rarely clear, articulated, and consistent. They're usually unspoken and they change based on the situation or the individual. Expectations are equally unclear and inconsistent. You're usually left to guess as to what constitutes "compliance" to the rules. Just when you think you've got it figured out, it's changed! So in that sense, the blame game is never executed on a level playing field! It always tilts away from you!

Is it any wonder why people within an anxious congregation develop creative strategies to avoid being blamed and accepting responsibility? In an anxious congregation you quickly learn that it's safer and easier if you keep your head down and your mouth shut. You get in less trouble that way! You stay on the sidelines, never get involved, never volunteer an opinion, just quietly occupy your

---

[7] Miller, 145

[8] Ibid., 149

[9] Ibid., 150

seat and avoid eye contact! Even if you're an extrovert like me!

You can see how the fear of risk and learning stand as intimidating and fearsome sentries guarding the anxious congregation from all it could be. I'm sure you recognize that it would take significant faith and courage to begin to speak into this kind of anxious reality. I think you'll also agree that is hardly what it looks like to love God and other people, at least the way Jesus intended! Anxious congregations are proficient at playing the blame game and identifying the scapegoat! In order to more constructively manage the relational anxiety and fear, these muscles must be exorcised and other muscles exercised, particularly those which enable each person to accept responsibility for his or her actions without a pervasive fear of retribution. Only then can they more freely seek to make constructive changes which will benefit the whole body!

Can We Three be "Friends"?

There's another common way in which anxiety manifests itself within an anxious congregation. If you've ever tried sitting on a two legged stool, you know it's an impossible task! It is hardly what you would call a "stable" piece of furniture. From my experience it would be akin to riding a unicycle, an impossibility for me!

Similar to a two-legged stool, a two person relationship can also be relatively unstable, unable to bear much in the way of tension or conflict without threatening to disrupt the "harmony" of the relationship and heighten the level of relational anxiety. If you and I are friends and tensions starts to build between us, it destabilizes the relationship. One of us will draw a third person into the relational matrix which results in an apparently more stable (and loving) relational dynamic. It's similar to adding a third leg to that two-legged stool in that it immediately brings stability!

The greater the anxiety and fear in a given relational system, the greater the propensity to create relational triangles. As and when anxiety increases, expect that existing triangles will birth new triangles. In anxious congregations the triangle fertility rate is extremely high and there's a very short gestation period! Typically, someone is always uncomfortable in a triangle and as a result pushes for change. Forming another triangle is often the preferred change option.

In a general sense, relational triangles serve a number of purposes. By bringing a third person into an unstable or anxious relationship, the triangle serves to absorb some of the anxiety. Now the focus doesn't need to be exclusively on the tension that exists between the two. It can be avoided as the three shift their focus elsewhere. Do not be fooled because the anxiety virus still infects the relational triangle even if it's not front and center! Nothing has been resolved! At best, the basic differences and conflicts have merely been covered over.

Another purpose served in the creation of triangles is closely related to blame and scapegoating. Assume again that I am in relationship with you. Tension starts to build which increases the level of anxiety and decreases the stability in the relationship. I go to a third person and say something like, "She sure is a negative person, always complaining about something. She's never happy! Little wonder she doesn't have many friends!" In an anxious congregation, it's extremely unlikely, in fact rare, that I would have come to you first with this concern. To do that, I would have to first deal with the anxiety and fear stirred up in me because of my uncertainty as to how you might respond. So rather than manage my own anxiety and fear, I have now "shared" it with a third person and have done so in a way that doesn't paint you in a particularly good light! Typically my motive will be to get the third person to agree with me about you. Remember, you're not present for the conversation or a part of it. If I can get the third person to agree with me that you're really a negative, complaining whiner, then we're halfway to solving the problem. You're the problem! So the "Christian" thing for you to do would be to recognize that God has spoken to the two of us, repent and be healed! My purpose in bringing in a third person is not to ultimately love God or love you better. It's to build an alliance. When I've successfully built that alliance, then you occupy the "odd one out" position in the triangle, which in turn is going to raise your anxiety level! There's a high likelihood that how you'll choose to manage that is to find a different third person that you can then draw into the relationship. Your conversation with them will go something like this, "Do you know what that Ken Thiessen did? He went and talked to so and so and they think I am a negative, complaining whiner!" Probably the third person you've drawn in will say something like, "Oh that's not true! How could he say that? What kind of a Christian would do that?" It's quite possible that your "friend" may actually agree with some of my assessment but is also afraid to be really honest with you so she patronizes you in her response. Now you have built an alliance which identifies me as the problem and another triangle has been formed. But how solid is your alliance or mine? It feels solid, but guess what, each of our "friends' will probably tell two friends, who'll tell two friends, who'll tell two friends and you've see the triangle birth rate sky-rocket faster that you can say the word "triangle".

Anxious congregations manifest a high level of proficiency in the "Can We Three Be Friends?" game. Triangles are the norm, not the exception. While the motivation on the surface appears to be a desire to love God and other people, the longer you find yourself engaged in a triangle, either in being drawn into one or by creating one yourself, the more you feel the inherent ugly and self-serving dynamics. They're counter-productive to truly loving God and other people the way Jesus envisioned it.

"Conversely, in healthier relationship systems, people do not spend their time with each other focusing negatively on an absent third person. Instead, they work toward building one-to-one relationship between them."[10] This kind of "can we three be friends" muscle needs to be exorcised and new muscles developed which enable the healthy development of two, three, four, five-person relationships where the focus is on building the one-to-one relationships within the group rather than talking disparagingly about an absent third party.

Saying "I" When Everyone Wants You to Say "We"

Anxious congregations also manifest a diminished proficiency for speaking in the first person. They're not very good at saying "I" and demonstrate a low level of tolerance when others say "I". In an anxious congregation it's almost always about the collective "we". "We believe, we think, we feel, we want, we're doing this, we've always done it this way, we're going there, this is our policy, this is our practise." I think you get the picture. What's interesting in an anxious congregation is that most people are content to let the collective "we" think, speak, and act for everyone else. And nobody questions anything! Oh, there's usually someone who's questioning internally, but rarely do they allow those questions to become audible.

---

[10] Ibid., 128

The Anxious Congregation

The reason? They've probably seen what happened to the last person who dared to question the collective "we"! The clan descended on the poor victim like piranhas on prey. The pressure exerted on the poor, unsuspecting victim to "see the light" and get onside with the group was immense. They probably caved in to the pressure and became a part of the collective "we" just like many others before them.

Anxious congregations are not comfortable with people who are able to self-differentiate and think, speak, feel, and act for themselves. It's deemed to be an unloving, disrespectful demonstration of disloyalty to the rest of the group to differ in even the slightest way! People who are able to think and speak for themselves represent a high level of risk and threat in an anxious congregation. The very notion that they might think differently than the rest raises the anxiety meter to frightening levels! As such, these independent thinkers must be silenced, forced to comply, or failing that, driven out!

Anxious congregations are not comfortable with, and have little room for debate. Debate brings with it the risk that no one person can control who says what. This has the potential of surfacing the anxiety already present, and quite likely intensifying it. Since anxiety is deemed harmful and detrimental to the collective "we" it must be stifled at all costs. One's appropriate (and peaceful) place in the group is secured by a willingness to comply and agree with the "we". Ongoing relationship is contingent on agreement and compliance, two of the predominant core values in an anxious congregation. Those who dare to think, feel, and speak for themselves are quickly labelled as troublemakers, malcontents, resistant to God and the Holy Spirit, and spiritually immature. That all under the guise of loving God and other people! That's not to say that occasionally there aren't some of those individuals within a given congregation. But anxious congregations are generous in their willingness to label any and all who would have the audacity to speak in the first person "I" rather than the collective "we".

The first person "I" muscle of self-differentiation is a muscle in desperate need of development, strengthening, conditioning, and toning in an anxious congregation! Not unlike a physio rehab routine, the rest of the body's "we" muscles will scream out in pain as this muscle is developed but its development is essential if the "we" muscles are to maintain a proportional and appropriate place and contribute to the healthy functioning of the body.

Fighting Fair

If blaming and scapegoating, triangulation, and an inability to facilitate and tolerate healthy self-differentiation are all problematic and in abundant supply in an anxious congregation, it should come as no surprise that conflict is also not handled well. It is rarely conducted in a fair and equitable manner that is respectful of all parties involved, which leads to any form of resolution of the underlying and deeper issues.

There are a number of ways in which anxious congregations fight. They don't. They fight from the bushes so you never really know who you're fighting. Or they're malicious and vindictive, sticking the proverbial knife in your back while hugging you and giving you the "love of the Lord" speech. None of these generally "accepted" approaches to dealing with conflict in an anxious congregation help facilitate the loving relationships with other people or with God that we're called to!

Learning to conflict in healthier, more loving ways is another muscle development, strengthening, and toning exercise that will facilitate a more productive and God-honouring way of managing the anxiety virus. The Apostle Paul is clear in his instruction to the Ephesian church. We are to stop lying and instead start speaking the truth in love to each other. That's the kind of behaviour that's consistent with those who profess a love for God and a commitment to live that out in the context of loving other people. The only way to exercise and develop this muscle is to move headlong into the anxiety, do the hard work of learning and developing new, more proactive and productive ways to conflict no matter how much the anxiety level spikes, no matter how intense the fear, and discover that there is life on the other side!

For Reflection and Discussion

1. In what ways do you contribute to the problem AND the solution in your congregation?

2. Of the various unhealthy strategies to manage anxiety identified in this chapter, which do you think are most prominent in your congregation? Which do you most naturally gravitate to personally? Why do you think that is? Which would be the most difficult to begin to address? For your congregation? For you personally?

3. What are some examples of where you have seen one or more of these at work in your congregation?

4. When you think of the power of one, what's the biggest hurdle you have to address to be the one who is a catalyst for positive change in your congregation?

Ken Thiessen

Chapter 15
Grenwich - Congregational Redesign

While the way Grenwich leadership functioned was starting to change, seeing change take place on a broader congregational level was a much slower, more deliberate process. There was no question Barry had started the ball rolling when he decided to stand up to David Hill. At the time he didn't realize how important that decision was, nor did he really know how much he was doing the "right" thing. But in hindsight, it had been the catalytic trigger of significant positive change for Grenwich. Time had given some perspective as to how many things he and others had done "right" in the process, and without any formal training at that. What they did possess was a deep and profound desire and commitment to love God and love others.

Momentum had built as the Board also took steps to challenge the status quo, illustrated in their response to David Hill and the events which ensued. It was also encouraging to see a growing group of people beginning to track with Barry in developing new ways of managing the underlying anxiety which had exerted so much influence on Grenwich for so long! It wasn't without its struggles and it didn't come without persistence and hard work. But there was a group who had stared down the fearless sentries of risk and learning. They had demonstrated faith and courage and had begun to break through the barrier which had firmly held Grenwich captive to its anxiety and fear. The leadership decided that the time had come to incorporate some of the changes into the broader mainstream of congregational life. They decided this could best be accomplished not by an edict from the Board or the pastor, or by a formal motion at a duly called congregational meeting, but by quietly and consistently changing the way each of them related to the rest of the system they knew as Grenwich. Rather than follow the "conventional" anxiety management practises which were so ingrained at Grenwich, they decided to go against the grain, defy (in a healthier way) the status quo, and begin to define a new "normal" for life at Grenwich.

Their first step was a decision to stop playing the blame game within the context of their leadership function and role. By now each of them knew the problem was bigger than David Hill. Individually, they also knew that they were complicit and part of the problem. They had enabled David Hill, allowing him to perpetuate his anxiety on the system, and had most often done so unknowingly. Their ignorance exposed, they had chosen to do the harder work of confession and repentance. They were slowly developing and implementing new ways of facing their fears and managing their anxiety. The relational template had been and continued to be retooled. They were fully engaged in the rehab process!

The blame game, however, was still very much alive and well within the larger congregation. More people were coming to leadership casting blame in a variety of directions, some at David Hill and others who were allied with him, some at the Board, some at Barry Moffat, and some at other individuals within the congregation. One by one, and as a group, the leadership began challenging those who found particular enjoyment in playing the blame game. Rather than using a full frontal attack, criticizing those casting blame and seeking to deflect responsibility, or challenging their assessment, the leadership used questions to stimulate ongoing thought and reflection. They reasoned that perhaps Jesus' penchant for well thought-out questions to surface deeper, more significant realities might be helpful as they sought to be catalysts for broader change among the congregation as a whole. Questions like, "Why do you believe that? In what way do you think this person is to blame or is responsible? In what way or ways do others share responsibility? In what way have you contributed to the problem? Who could have done something about this and didn't? Why didn't they do something? Who is best suited to speak into this situation? What might you do to be a part of the solution?" Just the fact that a question was raised was often enough to stop the other person dead in their tracks. It was not what they had expected by way of response! They had expected criticism, debate, defensiveness, or agreement, but not questions! The questions served to disarm the armchair critics and surface some of the underlying systemic anxiety in a way that gave opportunity for new and different ways of naming, owning, and managing it.

Not everyone was pleased, however. There were some who derived great personal enjoyment and satisfaction in playing the blame game but as they quickly came to realize, their playing days were coming to an end! There wouldn't be much room at Grenwich for the blame game to continue on unchallenged. They would need to find a new way to entertain themselves! Whether they realized it or not, they would be better off for it, and so would the rest of the congregation.

The second significant step leadership took in redesigning the way Grenwich lived life together as a congregation was to address the proliferation and perpetuation of relational triangles. They had come to recognize that David Hill's leadership style was dependent on relational triangles and building unhealthy alliances in order to get his way. Barry had courageously exposed the triangulation and had put the deeper issues on the table in a way that made it much more difficult for David to ignore them or control the outcome. It was harder for everyone else to ignore them too! It called David and others to deal with issues in a healthier way, something which David wasn't prepared to do. In raising the issues with the Board, Barry provided them an opportunity to set a new pattern in motion and deal with issues in an upfront, face to face manner. And they had!

In the process of dismantling the triangles which had influenced the interactions and decisions of Grenwich's leadership for a long time, the Board had begun to develop some new, much healthier ways of dealing with issues, ways which helped them more fully live out the call to love God and other people. On the congregational front however, addressing the proliferation of triangles proved a more daunting task that could best be addressed one triangle at a time. Since the prevalence of relational triangles was so pervasive, there was no shortage of opportunities to identify them, and call others to respond in new and more loving ways.

The approach leadership used to confront the unhealthy systemic dynamics was firm but gentle, and fair. It didn't matter who you were in the congregation, how long you had been at the church, to whom you were related, what your role in the church was, or how much money you gave to the ongoing support of the ministry. If you approached anybody in leadership to discuss your concerns about an absent third party, the response from leadership was consistent. "You should be talking directly to that person, not to me since this has nothing to do with me. If you are not comfortable going to talk to them alone, I'm prepared to go with you but I will not arrange it for you, nor speak for you. You will need to set it up and you will be the one speaking. If you want to go on your own, that's great. When do you plan to do that, and when can I expect a report back from you as to the outcome of your conversation? If I don't hear from you, I will be in touch with you to follow up. Would that be okay?"

Most who engaged in the perpetuation of relational triangles were taken aback by the new, unexpected response to what they knew to be "normal" in the context of Grenwich's life! The directness of the interaction and the new level of accountability made most of them extremely uncomfortable. It certainly didn't feel very loving, at least not how they defined love. But the leadership were convinced this was one tangible step they could model and call others to live by which would ultimately help them collectively live into the call to love God and love other people more fully.

Realizing that talking *about* people rather than *to* people was no longer going to work without being addressed in at least some quarters, people were now challenged to deal with the new reality and begin the process of developing new relational patterns. They were invited to do something many found quite radical, which was talk directly to people and build relationships that more closely fit the pattern of Scripture. There was no question this new relational paradigm involved what felt like risk. It also required learning, and the degree to which different people were able to live into that paradigm was in direct proportion to the level of their faith and courage. They were being called to live the deep change process and do so together as a congregation. Most importantly, the leadership were modelling for them what that actually looked like.

There were a couple of noticeable outcomes which manifested themselves in the broader scope of the life of the congregation. People actually started talking to each other about things that were important to them and that mattered to them and to Grenwich. While it was difficult at first, and it didn't go perfectly every time, they were at least stepping into the unknown, making the effort to love one another and love God. These interactions served to bring some of the underlying anxiety to the surface so that it could be named, owned, and managed in better ways. People also began to discover there was life on the other side! They could face their fears of how others would respond to them! The anxiety would not consume or destroy them! They could experience some level of mastery over it. The quality of their relationships could go so much deeper than what they ever dreamed possible!

There was a new creativity that began to emerge as individuals and groups of individuals came together to talk about life at Grenwich and the issues which were impacting the quality of community life. They talked much more intentionally about what it meant for them to love God, identifying specific ways in which they could do that more effectively. They began to brainstorm together in their efforts to develop new and more effective patterns of dealing with other issues affecting the people of Grenwich. Individuals who had previously been noticeably silent in any kind of group context soon emerged as reservoirs of creative wisdom and insight that served to stimulate further conversation, healthy dialogue, and even some debate! More importantly they interacted in ways that were respectful and transparent. Before long it wasn't just the leadership who were challenging those who wanted to perpetuate relational triangles. Other members of the congregation picked up the mantle and held each other accountable to love God and other people! Momentum was growing and change was slowly being realized.

The changing patterns of relational interaction surfaced other anxiety dynamics and issues needing to be addressed. As people began talking to rather than talking about one another, divergent opinions began to surface. This was a new experience for many since silent compliance had been one of the unspoken rules dictating these kinds of interactions. Ongoing relationship was contingent on agreement and compliance! If you didn't go with the flow, you were alienated and cut off relationally. The emerging question was, "What does it look like to love God and other people when we don't all agree?" What was that going to look like lived out at Grenwich in the new, emerging paradigm? Could people disagree and remain engaged relationally in a way that respected the differences and truly gave freedom for people to hold a dissenting or divergent opinion?

As more people engaged the changing relational patterns, they began to develop deeper, more meaningful and authentic friendships which were based on much more than compliant agreement. While the leadership had been learning that it was in fact possible to have divergent opinions, dialogue, and even debate, and maintain and grow solid relationships in the process, now others in the congregation were entering into that experience as well. There was a part of that experience that touched something deep within many, filling a longing that most had given up hope of ever experiencing in a meaningful and lasting way. Given that, it was not without its challenges as individuals grew into this new reality. They were exercising muscles that hadn't been exercised in a long time, and still other muscles they never knew existed!

As you might expect, with the increased freedom to express personal and divergent opinions, conflict surfaced. Not all of the divergent opinions were necessarily embraced by others. Some shouldn't have been embraced without some good dialogue and even debate. Learning how to debate with others in a wholesome and respectful way was at times a clumsy and awkward process. Things were said and attitudes conveyed that were not always loving, uplifting and productive. There was a temptation and tendency to resort to the old patterns of talking about people rather than to them as the conflict bubbled to the surface. They were learning that conflict would never go away, neither would the resulting anxiety. But what could change was the way in which they managed both! Usually others served as accountability barometers, calling individuals to deal with conflict in a manner that fit the parameters as laid out in Scripture, face to face, authentically and transparently speaking the truth in love, motivated by what was in the best interest of the individuals involved and the congregation as a whole, even if it was difficult and risky. The desired end goal was always constructive resolution and ongoing relational involvement. Sometimes this meant that the person "speaking the truth in love" had to accept the fact that what they thought was "loving" was in fact more about venting and self-protection than it was about truly acting out of a deep and abiding care for the other person. When that happened it was an opportunity to practise confession, repentance, and forgiveness.

While few questioned the biblical principles related to dealing with conflict, most agreed that consistently living out those principles was the ongoing challenge. And it would never go away! They would never be free of the hard work of relationships no matter how much they grew and matured spiritually. Just because their friendships were growing and were being built on a much more solid, biblical foundation didn't mean that conflict would go away, or that anxiety would completely dissipate. They held on to the notion that what would change were their strategies for managing conflict. They were walking a path that in some ways looked very different, but some parts of it would remain strangely familiar. The key was to keep walking, for better or for worse, together!

For Reflection and Discussion

1. What's your reaction to this chapter? Does it sound like a pipe dream or a real possibility for your congregation?

2. What parts of the chapter offer you and your congregation the most hope? Most discouragement? Most challenge?

3. Which of the changes implemented at Grenwich would be most difficult to implement in your congregation? Easiest? Which are you already doing, at least to some degree? What could you do to improve in those areas?

4. If the leadership in your congregation were to provide the kind of leadership demonstrated at Grenwich, how would people in your congregation respond?

5. What's the single most important change you could begin to make which would better help you manage your systemic anxiety and fear, and more fully love God and other people?

Chapter 16
Every Part Doing Its Part

If an anxious congregation like yours is seriously wrestling with the implications of the "follow me" call of Jesus, and is in increasing measure loving God and other people, what are some of the tangible, measurable expressions of positive progress? What road signs can you look for on your journey towards managing your anxiety and fear in ways that more fully equip and enable you to join God in mission in your local context?

As you read through the Apostle Paul's letter to the Corinthian church, you quickly discover a congregation whose anxiety was not well managed. It might be fair to say that the systemic anxiety was managing them and they weren't even aware of it! What they saw as a badge of honour was in fact a serious manifestation of the depth of their own self-deception! Paul reserves some of his most direct and confrontational comments for this church.

Based on a first read, it's not hard to imagine how some might take Paul's comments to be unloving and unduly harsh. But Paul's concern is motivated by the depth of his love for them and his concern about what's truly in their best interest. He says, "I am not writing these things to shame you, but to warn you as my beloved children. For even if you had ten thousand others to teach you about Christ, you have only one spiritual father. For I became your father in Christ Jesus when I preached the Good News to you. So I urge you to imitate me." (I Corinthians 4:14-16) Paul was prepared to risk having his motives and his true affections questioned in order to say what they most needed to hear!

Whatever concerns Paul had related to the Corinthian church, he was very clear on one thing. They were called of God, loved by God, and His Spirit was present in them. Of that Paul had no doubt and that was his starting point, his deep personal conviction, not just a perfunctory greeting.

Most congregations are more Corinthian than they realize, not only in the outworking of their life together, but also in their calling by God. They are called by God and are oftentimes naive as to the anxiety present and the degree to which it influences congregational life. In that sense Paul's letter provides a good backdrop for theological reflection related to the anxious congregation.

A review of Paul's letter reveals some of the issues present in the Corinthian church which caused Paul great concern. This was a deeply divided and factious group. Fuelled by their pride and arrogance, they rallied around personalities, ideologies, spiritual gifts and religious liberties. Their relational skills left much to be desired. They had poor or non-existent relational boundaries, didn't do conflict well, couldn't work things out among themselves, but instead resorted to lawsuits and the legal system to find resolution to issues. They were motivated more by self-interest than concern for others in the body, and were adept at identifying and establishing the hierarchical status pecking order within the congregation. Diversity was threatening and their sense of unity was based on the foundation of conformity. Nothing major. Just a couple of small issues! Whatever issues you face in your congregation, you should now realize that you're in relatively good company! There's at least one church that bears some similarity to yours!

Using the human body as a case study of sorts, Paul outlines some of the overarching principles which ought to guide a local congregation in its efforts to more fully love God and other people in response to the "follow me" call of Jesus. "The human body has many parts, but the many parts make up one whole body. So it is with the body of Christ." (1 Corinthians 12:12)

In the midst of all the divisions, factions, and controversies present in the Corinthian church, Paul reminds them that just as the human body is comprised of many unique and diverse parts, so too is the local church! The Corinthian local church! Your local church! Using that as his springboard, he begins to flesh that out for them, painting a picture of what it looks like lived out in the context of congregational body life.

Embracing Diversity - Many Parts, One Body

As an anxious congregation grows in its practice of loving God and other people, one of the visible indicators is the profound recognition that the many different, unique, and diverse individuals who are integrally connected within that congregation are each important and vital to the ongoing life of the congregation. Where a David Hill saw himself as first above equals, Paul says that's not the way it's designed to work in a congregation that has understood Jesus' "follow me" call and is living that out in growing measure.

Like the Corinthian church, anxious congregations typically find diversity a challenging and anxiety inducing reality. In their efforts to manage the anxiety, diversity is squelched and conformity is promoted as the sign and evidence of spiritual maturity and of being a part of the "team". You can imagine that the Corinthian church was not particularly impressed with Paul's direct and confrontational approach with them, just like most anxious congregations would not be impressed! Paul was challenging the status quo in a significant way! His sermon would have probably been met with mixed reviews, most less than endearing or positive! Would you blame them? When the mirror of 1 Corinthians is held up for your church to gaze into, do you find it a comforting exercise? Probably not! I suspect the anxiety thermometer would rise, approaching the boiling point!

Paul is very clear that diversity is something to be embraced, celebrated and championed in the life of a congregation that is effectively following Jesus on the path of loving God and other people! Where an anxious congregation works hard to minimize, squelch, and disparage diversity, Paul is emphatic that we see no such pattern in the human body, perhaps one of the better analogies of what congregational life ought to look like. There are many diverse parts but there is only one body and the health of the body is contingent on the diversity of parts. Squelching diversity, advocating conformity, elevating one part while minimizing other parts, transforms a beautiful creation into a mutated aberration of the Creator's original design. Paul says that anxiety left unchecked or managed poorly, is not God's design or desire for the people he gave his life for!

The other thing that Paul emphasizes quite strongly is the reality that in spite of the diversity that exists there is a profound sense of interdependence and interconnectedness within the human body. One part is intimately connected to the other. Many are dependent on the other for their ongoing wellbeing. Moreover, "if one part suffers, all the parts suffer with it, and if one part is honored, all the parts are glad." (1 Corinthians 12:26)

The Anxious Congregation

A personal example may be helpful. Due to a medical procedure on my heart, I developed a pulmonary embolism, a blood clot in my lung. I can assure you that my entire body felt the pain of that "small" little clot! I experienced pain unlike anything I had ever experienced before. Thanks to competent medical professionals and the wonders of modern medicine, I am alive to talk about it. Thirty to forty percent of people who share my experience are not so fortunate. There was no separating that clot or my lung from the rest of my body. They were intricately connected! My whole body knew it and experienced pain!

Not so in the Corinthian church! They lived as if this principle didn't apply to them. They showed little concern for the wellbeing of others within the body, little concern for how their actions might affect others. When one was honored, that gave rise to jealousy and envy, not celebration and enjoyment!

In an anxious congregation the tendency is to view the parts as independent, disconnected components. There is little regard for the inter-relationships that exist, how those inter-relationships impact the various component parts, or the effective functioning of the whole. What's more, in an anxious congregation component parts regularly and quickly detach themselves from the rest of the body without any apparent pain, or lingering consequence.

Go back to the analogy of the human body. When was the last time your arm decided to detach itself from your shoulder? If it did, do you think you'd notice? Would you feel anything? If you didn't, that would be a sure sign something much more serious was wrong! It's unthinkable, and you're probably shuddering at the thought of it! Any doctor who attempted to conduct that kind of limb amputation without anaesthetic would be considered cruel and abusive. Quite likely, he'd have his credentials to practise medicine withdrawn. I wonder then, why is that we treat the body of Christ, the local church, with such a high level of disrespect, thinking that we can recklessly separate component parts from the body without any sense of pain or consequence. There is a tendency to discard component parts as if they are yesterday's garbage, and we think we can continue on unaffected. So often it's a passionless, emotionless, painless process with no lingering consequence. Paul challenges that notion and it must give us pause for reflection. How can we say that is the best way, or even one way to live out the call to love God and other people?

Every Part Has a Part and Does Its Part

Paul is also emphatic that every part is important and every part has an important role to play in the functioning of the body. So too, in the church. There are no dispensable parts! There are no passive parts; no benchwarmers, no arm chair quarterbacks, no casual observers. That's not to say that at different points in time various body parts don't function in that capacity, but it's the exception rather than the norm. Importance is not measured on the basis of visibility, prominence, or size of the body part. Paul is clear that sometimes the obscure and small body parts deserve more attention, honor and care because they are more vulnerable. All body parts are essential and all body parts have a part to play in the ongoing, healthy functioning of the body.

Another significant analogy Paul draws out is the absolute dependence and interdependence which exists between the various body parts. One part can't say to the other, "I don't need you!" or vice versa. One part can't say to the others, "You need to be just like me!" There is a profound awareness that interdependence is critical and essential. Failure to exist interdependently is to hamper and limit the effective functioning of the body.

An anxious congregation finds this reality challenging to embrace, and balks at the thought of living into it. Anxious congregations are adept at elevating some body parts and diminishing others. Some body parts do the work of four or five other body parts, a phenomenon that the human body does not tolerate or condone! Warnings signs start flashing like huge red neon lights at the annual physical check-up if that is the case in the human body. Other body parts start "screaming" out in reaction!

Not so in the anxious congregation. The over-functioning body parts in the anxious congregation are often times held up as models of spiritual maturity and commitment when in fact they ought to be diagnosed as unhealthy and not well! For every congregational body part that is running around doing the work of four or five other body parts, you have a host of body parts sitting comfortably on the sideline doing nothing! Those body parts ought to be rebuked for their inactivity! The whole body functions best when every part does its part, no more, and no less! When and where a human body part begins compensating for another under-functioning body part it's almost always an indication that something is wrong. It's definitely not something to be applauded and celebrated.

Another important reality within the human body is how various body parts spring into action to maintain and preserve the healthy functioning of the entire body when attacked by a destructive external source. If my body is attacked by a virus, the defence mechanisms of my body immediately kick into gear in an effort to fight off the virus. If the body either ignores the virus, or is incapable of fighting the virus, that's usually a sign of something much more serious going on, such as an immune deficiency, cancerous cells, or another body part not functioning at or near full capacity. Nonetheless, the body has an internal built-in fight and warning mechanism which kicks into gear. When the body's defence mechanisms are unable to fight off the attack and the symptoms prolong or worsen, we make a visit to our medical doctor who diagnoses the situation and prescribes a treatment regimen. Sometimes, based on our anxiety and fear related to the unknown nature of what's going on in our bodies, we avoid going to the doctor rather than manage the anxiety and receive treatment. That's rarely helpful. The problem rarely goes away!

In an anxious congregation, the built-in fight and warning mechanism is significantly stunted, if active at all. Most often, the underlying realities are ignored or suppressed, and life continues on as "normal". I am aware of numerous situations where two individuals have been at odds for decades all the while "peacefully" co-existing in the same congregation. They sit on opposite sides of the church at worship and avoid each other in social gatherings. Social gatherings are planned so as to ensure they're never invited to the same event. No one can remember what the precipitating issue was, they just know there's a "problem" and everyone avoids addressing the issue. One of the parties projects a fragility that insulates them from ever being confronted. Others are firmly convinced the individual would be crushed by even the most gentle of attempts to broach the subject, so they ignore it, strangely hoping it will go away! In a surprising way, the "weakest" person in the situation wields the most power! All in all, no one is prepared to manage their own anxiety in an effort to speak redemptively into the situation and in the process they enable the ongoing dysfunction. It's no longer about the two affected parties, but it's about the functioning of the entire body!

Imagine what that might look like in the human body. "You know for thirty years my heart and my lungs have not been able to get along. Not sure what caused it, but they avoid each other. Every time I try to bring it up and find out what's going on my heart starts racing like I'm about to have a heart attack and that's the end of it." That kind of scenario would never occur in the human body. In fact when it's spelled that way we see how ludicrous it really is! However, more often than not it's common place in the anxious congregation. Paul has something to say to that. This should not be!

Anxious congregations don't look beyond themselves to discover the ways in which anxiety is at work in their life together, or make an effort to learn and develop more effective and godly ways of managing the anxiety. They are often unaware of the seriousness of the problem and too proud to admit that they require outside help to address the internal realities which are negatively affecting body life. To bring in an external resource would be to admit failure, give up control. They are afraid of the "diagnosis" and what might be required of them to get "well" so they avoid it. They fear that maybe they're worse off than they imagine, or that perhaps their worst fears will be realized.

Unity and Diversity - Not Mutually Exclusive

In addressing the Corinthian church Paul celebrates diversity and champions it as a value to be pursued. Using the human body as the analogy, he illustrates how diversity and unity can coexist in the same body without one infringing on the other, without one consuming the other. In fact, their unity finds its most fruitful expression in the context of diversity! In highlighting this he challenges an underlying issue in the Corinthian congregation. They were uncomfortable with diversity and saw it as a threat to their unity. As a result, their modus operandi was to advocate conformity and compliance as the norm, as the route to "true" unity. Paul exposes their naiveté as pure, baseless myth. He convincingly suggests instead that the very thing they see as a threat to their unity is in fact the means to most fully experience it! Diversity and unity are not mutually exclusive! They can coexist within the same congregation!

Anxious congregations are strong proponents and advocates for conformity and compliance. In their congregational paradigm, unity and relationship is contingent on it! To compromise on conformity and compliance is to invite disunity and division. Ironically, it was in advocating conformity that the Corinthian church most experienced disunity and division! If Jesus' "follow me" call is a call to love God and other people more passionately and do so with the sum total of our being, then I can't imagine a better way of illustrating what that looks like than in the context of a diverse group of people who comprise a given local congregation. I didn't say it would be easy, but I can't think of a better example! It's much easier to love people who think like you, believe like you, and act like you. It's much more challenging to love those who are different than you. Just ask Jesus' disciples!

In my experience, anxious pastors who provide leadership in anxious congregations fail to do what Barry Moffat did, and surround themselves with strong, diverse leaders! Most pastors find the thought of this to be a frightening exercise! They are intimidated and afraid, which are hallmarks of anxiety! They're afraid that these strong leaders might hold a mirror up in front of them, exposing areas where he or she might not be loving God or other people as fully as they could. Behind their fear is a deep-seated insecurity that they might not have all the answers. But what they fail to realize is they limit their own growth as a leader; they fail to most fully live out God's call to love other people, and the quality of their decision-making and leadership influence are diminished. A team of strong, gifted and diverse leaders who have learned how to relate in ways that model the interdependence and interconnectedness that Paul references in his letter to the Corinthian church are a gift to an anxious congregation. They illustrate the principle that unity and diversity are not mutually exclusive. A congregation like Grenwich benefited from the strong leadership team that assembled in the wake of the upheaval! The entire congregation was the beneficiary of the unity they experienced in the midst of great diversity. Where an anxious congregation runs in fear from diversity, it ought instead to embrace and celebrate it in all its fullness, recognizing the sheer beauty that emerges when a diverse group of people love God and love each other and do it well!

No Dispensable Parts - Really?

There is one final point to address in the context of Paul's address to the Corinthian church. Paul's choice of the human body as the analogy for understanding congregational life presents one small challenge. As much as Paul stands on the notion that all parts are essential and none are dispensable, the reality is that some parts of the human body are apparently "dispensable". I, for example, function quite fine (if I can accurately be the arbiter of that) without a gall bladder or tonsils. I know others who function without a spleen, kidney, lung, appendix, or part of a liver. That's not to say that the rest of the body doesn't compensate in some way, but it still presents a challenge in terms of understanding Paul's analogy.

I'm told that while I might think I live fine without a gall bladder, other organs pick up some of the function of the gall bladder. Where other organs are removed from a human body, oftentimes drugs are required to compensate for the absence of the particular organ. The spleen is one example of this. The one organ that many are unsure of as to its usefulness is the appendix. There is no need for ongoing medication following the removal of the appendix, and no apparent compensatory behaviour on the part of other organs. Perhaps the appendix was an "afterthought" in the creative process. I'm not sure I want to go down that path!

So how are we to attempt to reconcile this in the context of understanding Paul and applying the principles to congregational life? I agree with the psalmist who affirms that we are fearfully and wonderfully made! We are complex creatures and I don't believe the appendix was an afterthought of God in the creative process. Nor is the "appendix" in your anxious congregation! Like Paul, I affirm that all parts of the body are important and necessary in the functioning of the body whether that is the human body or the body of Christ which finds expression in an anxious, local congregation.

In the human body, it's true that life can continue on without the presence of some body parts. However, that was never God's original design or intent. When and where a body part is deemed "expendable" it's always precipitated by a malfunction of one sort or another by that particular organ. The removal of that organ is always a means of last resort. I had gall bladder attacks for an extended period of time which served notice that the healthy functioning of my gall bladder was starting to break down. When the frequency and intensity of the attacks became more pronounced, doctors decided to remove the affected organ. I have been symptom free ever since! If someone were to choose to have elective surgery to remove a fully functioning body organ, we would look at them with some suspicion and concern. That's not usual behaviour for "normal" people.

How does Paul's analogy then carry over to the context of an anxious congregation? Are there in fact "dispensable" body parts in an anxious congregation, and if so, who determines which parts are dispensable? Paul speaks to this reality as well in confronting the Corinthian church on their prideful tolerance of sin. A man who was considered to be a part of the church was living in sin with his stepmother and the Corinthians did nothing to confront it. In fact they prided themselves on their "love" for this man! Paul's solution? "Then you must throw this man out and hand him over to Satan so that his sinful nature will be destroyed and he will be saved on the day the Lord returns." (I Corinthians 5:5) An apparent dispensable body part in the Corinthian church!

Scripture is silent in terms of all that had transpired prior to Paul's address of the issue, but it would be reasonable to assume there was no doubt or question as to the inappropriate nature of this man's conduct or the tolerance level of the Corinthian church. This kind of conduct, Paul suggests, was deemed unacceptable by "pagans" who didn't embrace or live according to the same spiritual values the Corinthians purported to embrace and live according to. At the point of Paul addressing the issue, the ongoing presence of this man in the Corinthian church constituted a threat to its long-term wellbeing and Paul deemed it appropriate that other body parts spring into action to protect the integrity of the body, fighting off the virus attacking its very lifeblood. The method Paul advocated was a very public, communal, and decisive confrontation of the issue.

Jesus addressed a similar kind of situation in Matthew 18. Speaking to the matter of relational conflict and "sin" he lays out a process for addressing it. Incorporated into that process is the extreme measure of treating that person "as a pagan or a corrupt tax collector". (Matthew 18:17) In other words, have nothing to do with them! But an important caveat is in order. It too is the means of last resort. Three steps precede this decisive action. Go to the person privately. If they do not, listen take two or three others, and if they still do not listen, take it to the church. If they STILL do not listen, then treat them as a pagan or corrupt tax collector. The goal of each step in the process is reconciliation and restoration. There is increased level of communal involvement before the decisive action is taken so there is always a relational component to it. More importantly, it is the body that makes the final decision not the "body part".

How does this speak into the experience of an anxious congregation? Often in anxious congregations, it's the body part that decides it is dispensable. Figuratively, the gall bladder says to the rest of the body, "see ya!" That is inconsistent with both the Corinthian and the Matthew contexts! Anxious congregations typically dispense with body parts in an underhanded and behind the scenes manner. Usually the basis for deeming a body part dispensable has much more to do with non-conformity and non-compliance to the rules of anxious engagement than it has to do with a consistent, persistent violation of a clear biblical principle. And it's rarely done in way that involves multiple levels of relational engagement with the rest of the body! Anxious congregations typically avoid Jesus' approach outlined in Matthew 18. To do that would be to heighten the level of anxiety and the reasoning is that heightened anxiety is never right, loving or Christian!

What principles might come into play then as an anxious congregation seeks to live out Paul's call in their local context?

First, God's design is that each part is important and each part has a role to play in the effective functioning of a local congregation. However, we seek to live out God's call in the context of a world that is broken and tainted by sin, ours, others, and the collective sin of the anxious congregation. The implication is that some "body parts" will not function according to their original intended design. They will sometimes resist any and all efforts by the rest of the body to bring them back into greater alignment with the original design. When and where an individual body part professes allegiance to Christ and claims a commitment to live out Jesus' "follow me" call to love God and other people, and repeatedly refuses the community's call to live consistent with that stated profession, then, and only then should the congregation give serious consideration to more drastic and decisive action. It must always be done in an up-front manner, with an obsessive emphasis on involvement from the broader community. It must be the means of last resort, implemented only after all other options have been exhausted. The door for re-entry must always be left open should the individual choose to confess and repent of their actions. Implementing these principles will itself be anxiety–inducing; it will not be easy, nor should it be. But the overall health of the body depends on it so the anxiety must be acknowledged, managed and embraced. As Paul reiterates, an anxious congregation never engages a process of this magnitude on its own, but does so under the influence, empowerment, and sanction of the Holy Spirit.

For Reflection and Discussion

1. On a scale of 1 to 10 (1 being low, 10 being high) how much is your congregation able to truly embrace and celebrate the diversity that characterizes your church?

2. What helps you embrace and celebrate your diversity? What makes it more difficult?

3. What is your congregation's pattern of dealing with people who leave? In what ways would you say your pattern is healthy? Unhealthy? What adjustments might you need to make to better love God and other people?

4. How does your congregation respond to the over-functioners who do the work of three, four, or five "body parts"? How does your congregation respond to the under-functioners who are content to sit on the sidelines and allow the over-functioners to their thing?

5. If, as Ken suggests, the body as a whole were more involved in the process of people leaving, how do you think that would impact your congregation? How hard would it be to implement that process? Why do you think that is?

Chapter 17
Grenwich - Still Anxious But Self Aware

As Grenwich continued to grow in their ability to love God and other people, they began to more quickly embrace the anxiety which they realized was inherent to the life of every congregation. They were less bound by their fears, which were still plentiful. They were getting more comfortable with accepting and celebrating the diversity reflected in the congregation, and relationships were growing deeper as they resorted to healthier patterns of interaction. They were also growing in their realization that anxiety in and of itself wasn't good or bad, right or wrong. It was more about how they managed their anxiety that determined the appropriateness of it. They were also growing in their self-awareness of anxiety's presence and its impact on their life together.

While they were growing spiritually as a congregation, they were also continuing to experience numerical growth. The upheaval with David Hill had put previous facility expansion plans on hold, but they found themselves in a position where they could no longer ignore their space limitations and challenges. They appointed another Building Committee to once again explore their options. The Committee was given the mandate to explore expansion on their current site, purchase existing retail space and renovate, or relocate to a new location and build a brand new facility. They were asked to explore each of the options and come back to the congregation with a report and recommendation. Barry decided that he would not be a member of this committee and informed Chris Graham accordingly. It wasn't that he didn't have an interest in their work, or didn't have something to offer. He knew that his primary calling was to provide pastoral leadership to the congregation and he needed to remain focused on that as his greatest priority. He also knew the Building Committee was comprised of very qualified and gifted people, and he was confident they would do excellent work on their own. As such, they didn't need him.

Coincidental with addressing the facility limitations, the Board made another significant decision that would have a profound impact on the spiritual growth of the congregation. As they had begun to more clearly articulate the values that would shape and govern life within Grenwich, one of the values identified was leadership development. Each member of the Board realized they had accepted their role with little in the way of formal training. There was no ongoing process for equipping existing leaders and developing future leaders. When they reviewed the congregation's budget, there was no money allocated for leadership development. The Board came to the congregation with the recommendation that if leadership development was really one of the values they were committed to living out, then that needed to be reflected in their annual budgeting process, and they needed to develop a conscious plan of developing leaders. The congregation heartily endorsed the recommendation and approved the revised budget.

Barry and the Board began developing a plan for ongoing leadership development and agreed to an annual leadership development event sponsored by someone other than Grenwich. They believed they could benefit from hearing what other leadership experts had to say, and they believed it was important they attend these events as an entire leadership team. They agreed on an event to attend and made plans to extend the invitation beyond elected Board members.

Their first experience participating in a leadership development conference whet their appetites in ways they could never have dreamed possible. Under Barry's and Chris's leadership they decided to intentionally debrief each of the sessions as a leadership team. Their focus was on applying what they had heard to the context at Grenwich. The relationship building, assessment and evaluation of what they were currently doing or not doing, dialoguing about potential or required changes and modifications to their existing approach to ministry, and the honest self-reflection began to reap significant benefits for them as a leadership group and the congregation as a whole. The investment in leadership development would prove to be one of the more significant financial and transformational decisions the congregation had made! In the process they had begun to change the leadership paradigm and the corresponding expectations of those who would hold leadership positions in the congregation.

As the Building Committee continued their due diligence process, they left no stone unturned. Their work completed to the point where they felt comfortable reporting back to the congregation, a meeting was scheduled. The Chair of the Building Committee provided a comprehensive report addressing the pros and cons of each option considered. When it came time for a recommendation the Building Committee suggested that relocating to a new location, a bare piece of land, would be the most fiscally responsible decision given all the information they had gleaned in their due diligence process.

Chris Graham, Board Chair, called for a coffee break in the meeting indicating that a formal vote on the recommendation would take place upon reconvening the meeting. During the break, Chris was approached by an individual who had begun attending Grenwich around the time things came to a head with David Hill but had never formalized the relationship with the church through membership. He owned a number of different properties in the community and informed Chris that should the congregation choose to relocate to a bare piece of land, he was prepared to donate the land required for a new building. Chris was taken aback by the generosity of this individual, thanked him for it but agreed that he would not divulge this information until after the vote. When the vote was conducted the overwhelming majority voted in favour of the Building Committee's recommendation to relocate. Only then did Chris Graham inform the congregation that he had received an offer of land for the new building, donated at no cost to the church and with no strings attached! Where David Hill had used his money as a club in an effort to beat the congregation into submission, God had graciously replaced it with something that amounted to much more than what David Hill had promised to give.

Word quickly spread throughout the community that Grenwich had voted to relocate and build a brand new facility that would not only house their ministry but would also serve as a facility the community could use! The process of seeing that plan realized had several hurdles attached to it, the first of which was securing the sale of their existing meeting space. They knew this was not going to be an easy process. There wasn't a huge resale market for existing church buildings. If they were going to get fair market value for it that would most likely be realized in a sale to another church in the community.

Barry received a call at the church office not long after from a city councillor who attended another church in the community. The purpose of his call was to inquire as to the accuracy of the reports circulating through the community related to Grenwich's decision to relocate. When Barry confirmed the reports to be true, the councillor indicated that the congregation he was a member of would be interested in engaging serious negotiation for the purchase of the building. Unsolicited, without even contacting a realtor, there was serious interest in the purchase of the building! The leadership had already determined what they believed to be fair market value of the building, so Barry referred this gentleman to Chris Graham to continue the discussion. Without much negotiation at all, the other congregation offered Grenwich what they had already deemed to be fair market value! Was this just coincidence or was God in fact honouring the many steps they had taken on their journey to love Him and other people more faithfully and more intentionally? They weren't sure, but they weren't about to question it either!

The formal offer to purchase precipitated another significant decision for Grenwich. They had no approved design for a new building, and had at best a budget figure as to what construction costs might be, but they had no idea as to what they might realize by way of a formal capital fundraising campaign. But they had a formal offer to purchase which required a response. There were lots of legitimate reasons for anxiety as their decision would set them on a course of action with plenty of unknowns. That brought with it varying degrees of fear on the part of individuals within the congregation. But when all was said and done, the congregation voted overwhelmingly to accept the offer to purchase. There was a real sense in which they were now homeless! They had crossed the point of no return. They were moving forward whether they liked it or not, and they were taking their anxiety along for the ride. Perhaps more importantly, they had broken the historic pattern at Grenwich of going with what was safe, with what they knew they could handle! They had demonstrated faith and courage in order to risk and learn!

As the Building Committee went to work on a design for the new building, they opted for an innovative, energy efficient building. While it was unconventional and daring, they presented the plan to the congregation along with a more comprehensive construction budget. The congregation was intrigued and inspired by the design concept and again, overwhelmingly approved the design, although not without some resistance from some surprising quarters. There were a small group of individuals who could not see themselves clear to support the expense of money to build a new facility. This was about to test the substance of the growth which Grenwich had experienced in terms of how they dealt with diversity, conflict, and disagreement. The Board followed through on their earlier practise of meeting with individuals who were contemplating leaving or had left. Several families felt they needed to leave, so members of the Board met with them.

One meeting was particularly difficult because the family leaving were close personal friends of Barry and Diane. As they met with the leadership there was no animosity or hostility, just plenty of tears. These were not enemies who were leaving, these were friends. The leadership assured the couple that should they ever choose to return, the door would be open for them and they would be welcomed back with open arms. A meaningful time of prayer ensued and they parted the way they had entered the meeting, as friends.

As the leadership began the process of a formal capital fundraising campaign, they secured the services of an external consultant with expertise in assisting congregations raise funding. The primary focus of the campaign was more about ministry and stewardship than it was about money and buildings. The leadership had been clear that the building was a tool for ministry not an edifice to be treated as a shrine. There was strong involvement from the congregation and the consultant provided the leadership with some scenarios as to what they might realize in a campaign of this sort, given his experience in other contexts. When all was said and done, the amount pledged came in significantly lower than what had been anticipated, which served to raise the anxiety level of many in leadership. But there was no turning back. They needed to proceed.

Six months later they broke ground on the construction of a new building on ten acres of donated land! The design itself generated a lot of conversation in the community, with many curious onlookers coming by to see it take shape. What Grenwich hadn't factored into the equation was a significant construction boom which escalated construction costs by 30%. Once the shovels had broken ground they had to keep going. Another reason for anxiety to spike. Another opportunity to apply better anxiety management skills. Another opportunity to demonstrate faith and courage!

Just as they had broken ground on the new building Chris Graham received a call from Barry Moffat asking if they could have lunch. When they met, Barry informed Chris that he had received an invitation to consider applying for another ministry position, something which Barry was ideally suited for. Barry shared his sense of angst about leaving Grenwich just as they were heading into a major building project. All the ministry textbooks said this was probably the worst time for a pastor to leave the congregation. Given Barry and Chris's relationship, Barry felt comfortable having the conversation with Chris and getting his perspective on it. Chris shared his affirmation that the ministry opportunity would suit Barry's gifts and skill set well, and assured him that if God was indeed calling him to this, Chris would not stand in the way, nor would the church. Both Barry and Chris were able to name and own their individual anxiety in the situation but agreed that if God was indeed calling Barry to move on, he would provide Grenwich all they needed to continue their journey and do so faithfully. Within a few short months, and before the building was completed, Barry informed the congregation that he had in fact accepted a call to another ministry position and would be leaving. There was genuine sadness at his leaving because he had been such an important catalyst for positive change in the midst of a very challenging and difficult period in Grenwich's history. But it was providing a new opportunity for them to face their fears and continue to grow in their abilities to manage their anxiety in ways that trusted God and continued to follow his call to love him and other people more passionately and more intensely.

Six months after Barry and Diane relocated, the church moved into the new building to lots of excitement, anticipation and apprehension. They had a larger mortgage than anticipated, had just called a new pastor, but they were reasonably certain that God was not going to abandon them. As they planned their formal service of dedication they extended an invitation to Barry and Diane to join them for the service, which they quickly agreed to do. They were excited to be able to return to a place that had yielded many significant friendships and personal spiritual growth. Their time together had been transformational, although not without significant growing pains and intense struggle. Together they had learned much about anxiety, individually and collectively. Together they had faced many of their individual and collective fears. They had learned so much about what it really meant to love God and love each other. They realized much more fully the cost of responding to Jesus' "follow me" call. They had come out the other side of the turmoil surrounding David Hill with a much greater appreciation for who God was, how he was at work in their lives, and they had experienced some of the fruit of the struggle. God had been faithful. Their anxiety had not got the best of them, but it hadn't gone away either. They had not been held captive to their fears and they knew they would still have to face new and different fears. But they had learned how to manage it in more productive and healthy ways and keep moving forward in spite of the fear and anxiety.

For Reflection and Discussion

1. As you read the ongoing story of Grenwich, what thoughts or feelings surface for you?

2. What do you see as some of the more significant factors which helped shape the way in which Grenwich's story has unfolded?

3. If bringing deeper, systemic change is really about the power of one, from a human perspective who is the one person who acted as the catalyst for positive change and growth at Grenwich? What price did that person have to pay? Why do you think they were able to pay that price?

4. If you had been a member of the leadership team at Grenwich, how do you think you would have responded to the challenges they experienced? What decisions and/or changes would you have found most difficult? What

decisions and/or changes do you think would be most difficult for your congregation?

5. What lessons do you take from their experience as it relates to your congregation?

Chapter 18
Your Congregation - On Mission with God

We began this journey with a question. Is your congregation an anxious congregation? If it was, how would you know? What if it was and you just didn't realize it? What criteria would you use to frame your response? I told you I'd see you on the other end. Well, here we are. At least I'm here and I sincerely hope you are too! Hopefully, like Barry Moffat, you've discovered there is life on the other side!

So, where to from here? You now have a bit more information than you did when we began this journey. Hopefully you've been stimulated to reflect theologically as you interacted not only with the story of Grenwich but also the teaching of Scripture. You are now responsible for the information you've gained along the way. My primary goal is not just to provide information but to be a catalyst for theological reflection that leads to transformation.

I suspect by now you have come to the realization that your congregation is in fact an anxious congregation. There are fears which hold you captive and inhibit your ability to fully respond to Jesus' "follow me!" call. You are an anxious pastor, church leader and congregant. You too have fears which fuel your anxiety. I hope by now you also realize you are not alone. You are not unique. Your experience of congregational life is not completely unique. Your ministry context will always have unique aspects to it, but the dynamics of congregational life have some remarkable similarities and patterns. Grenwich's story is probably your story in more ways than you care to admit.

I have a good friend who specializes in transitional ministry, working with anxious congregations who have gone though a particularly difficult period of conflict and turmoil. He will often call and we will engage in conversation about the current church in which he is ministering. As he begins to share some general observations, and without knowing the specifics of each church he works with, on more than one occasion I have said to him, "I suspect this is what you're also encountering" and I will then go into more detail as to what my hunch is. Often he has said to me, "How did you know that? Are you reading my mail?" There are some predictable patterns that manifest themselves in anxious congregations, your anxious congregation. That doesn't make you a bad person, a bad pastor, a bad church leader, or a bad church!

Just as Paul could affirm his deep conviction that the Corinthian church was called of God and loved of God, I affirm that about you as well! If you are reading this book I believe you are relatively serious about responding affirmatively to Jesus' "follow me" call to love God and other people, and to do so with the sum total of your being. I believe that you want to grow in not only your understanding of what that means, but also your ability to live into that understanding in increasing measure. I know you're probably apprehensive about what it will cost you. You're probably afraid. Remember, you will have to stare down the fearsome sentries of risk and learning. That will require faith and courage. Some days, perhaps many days, you won't think you have what it takes. Risk it anyway!!!

What's the best way to do that? Do what Barry Moffat did. Don't embark on the journey alone. Bring someone else with you. Like they say, misery loves company! I really don't mean that but there is truth to the axiom. Gather a group of others together and invite them to read the book with you. More than that, engage in discussion of the study questions at the end of each chapter. Focus not on some hypothetical church like Grenwich. Focus on your anxious congregation. Risk asking these questions of your congregation. Risk being brutally honest and transparent! Admit that you have a problem. Ask God for help to deal with whatever it is he reveals to you as you take stock of your fearless moral inventory. Ask him to show you specific ways in which anxiety is present in your congregation, ways in which you could better manage your fear, and ways in which you could more fully love him and one another. I guarantee he's going to answer every one of those prayers! Why? Because I know he has your best interests at heart! He wants what's best for you! He loves you!

If you don't already have a formal leadership development program in place, you might want to implement one. Whichever route you choose to go, make sure your leadership engage it as a group, and participate in a formal debrief of the learning experience with a special emphasis on applying what you're learning to your local congregational context. There is no substitute for an intentional, disciplined, and regular program of leadership development. Recruit gifted and diverse people to be involved in this process. It may make it more challenging but you'll reap the benefits of it down the road, if you continue to value and celebrate that diversity.

You might want to consider bringing in an external resource person, not an expert, but someone with expertise. You are the expert related to your congregation and your ministry context.

However, since you are so much a part of the anxious congregation, you can't see things as clearly as someone who comes in from the outside. They will probably ask questions you're either afraid to ask, haven't thought of asking, or have stopped asking! Your particular denomination may have resource people who could be a resource to you similar to what Grenwich discovered. Don't allow your pride to stand in the way of your congregation becoming all it could be and all God wants it to be.

Lastly, get comfortable with your anxiety. Name your fears. Face them! They're not going away! They're always going to be a part of your experience of life together. If you're serious about responding to Jesus' "follow me" call, it's always going to stretch you and take you to places where your anxiety will go before you. You will be afraid. If you're not anxious about where God's calling you to go, then it's probably not God's call you've responded to. Even people of profound faith feel anxious. The issue is whether they're going to manage their fear and anxiety and move forward anyway, or allow the fear and anxiety to manage them, keeping them immobilized where they're at.

Remember the picture of the disciples on the boat in the middle of the storm with Jesus sound asleep! They were terrified, assured that their lives were rapidly coming to an end. Jesus' response to them was, "Why are you so afraid? Have you no faith?" Your boat may be out on the water in the middle of a huge storm, but as long as Jesus is in the boat with you, you're okay! Keep following. Keep wrestling with what it means to love God and other people with the sum total of your being. Then do as you please! You'll probably be okay! But never give up!

For Reflection and Discussion

1. As you reflect back on the journey you began as you started reading, what are your thoughts and feelings? Are you glad you responded to the invitation? Sorry you did? Why do you think that is?

2. What's the biggest thing you've learned about yourself as you've read the book? About your congregation?

3. What are some of the key things God has been speaking to you personally as you've read? What's he saying to your congregation?

4. Review your definition of an anxious congregation at the beginning of the book. Would you change the definition at all? If so how?

5. What does God want to do in you as a result of what you've learned in this process? What does he want to do in your congregation? What are some of the challenges you face as you consider responding to God's "follow me" call now? What are some of the challenges your congregation faces?

6. What is your most important "next step" to act on what you now know? Personally? As a congregation?

Ken Thiessen

Chapter 19
Grenwich - An Update

I can imagine you'd like to know what's become of Grenwich Community Church. The church continued to experience growth under new pastoral leadership. They grew spiritually and they grew numerically. Three years after they moved into their new building, they received an unexpected letter in the mail. It came from an attorney informing them that Grenwich had been named as a 1/3 beneficiary of a sizeable estate. The deceased individual had been a member of the congregation long before any of the current leadership had begun attending the church. Grenwich's portion of the estate amounted to approximately 40% of the original construction cost of their new facility. Barry had heard rumours of this prior to his leaving, but none of the current leadership had any idea this was about to land on their doorstep. Had they known this sooner, it might have eased some of their anxiety and fears but for whatever reason, God chose to keep that from them.

Ironically the new pastor who followed Barry was not someone who was as free to name his anxiety and fears and own them. His fears managed him more than he managed them. As the leadership began working with him he became increasingly resistant to input, and anger started to manifest itself. After extensive unsuccessful efforts to work redemptively with him, he resigned and moved on to another church. Grenwich went through a period of significant upheaval in the process and some of the key leaders stepped back. They had led Grenwich through a significant period of transition following the David Hill scenario and they felt they needed a sabbatical of sorts. Some determined that the price of managing anxiety well was more than they were willing to pay, and they let their guard down. Other David Hill types stepped back into the mix and Grenwich has returned to some of its earlier unhealthy patterns of managing anxiety.

Not all is lost though. A new group of Barry Moffats are emerging from within the congregation and there is hope, but they are embarking on another journey. With the help of a transitional pastor they have begun that journey. They are hopeful but apprehensive, not sure if they have what it takes to persist. They're afraid of the future but they're moving into it anyway, believing that "he who began a good work in you will be faithful to complete it."

For Reflection and Discussion

1. What's your reaction to Grenwich's current reality? Does it leave you discouraged? Surprised? Without hope in your current situation?

2. Why do you think a church under a leadership team who had demonstrated such faith and courage would fall back into old patterns related to anxiety and fear?

3. What factors might have contributed to the regression they experienced?

4. What further lessons can you learn from Grenwich's experience?

5. As you think about your own journey as a congregation, what kinds of things can you do in an effort to reduce the risk of falling back into your old patterns once you've developed new patterns?

ABOUT THE AUTHOR

Ken Thiessen is the Senior Consulting Partner of Power of One Consulting. He lives together with his wife Bev in Regina, Saskatchewan. A graduate of Providence College and Seminary (Otterburne, MB) (B.A./M. Div.) he completed a Doctor of Ministry degree at Carey Theological College (Vancouver, B.C.) in 2008. His Doctoral Project, "Exploring the Use of Power in the Health of the Congregational System" was seminal in framing his thoughts for The Anxious Congregation. He is a certified coach with Gazelles International and consults executive teams and boards of growth-oriented churches, nonprofit organizations, and businesses in strategic planning, organizational health and development, and team building. He also conducts a one day **The Anxious Congregation** Workshop. For more information visit the website or contact him by email.

Web - www.powerofoneconsulting.ca
Email - ken@powerofoneconsulting.ca

www.ingramcontent.com/pod-product-compliance
Lightning Source LLC
Chambersburg PA
CBHW032042150426
43194CB00006B/389